Dictionary of Science

Dictionary of Science

Bhawani Kumar

Published by
PRABHAT PRAKASHAN PVT. LTD.
4/19 Asaf Ali Road,
New Delhi-110 002 (INDIA)
e-mail: prabhatbooks@gmail.com

ISBN 978-93-5048-507-1
DICTIONARY OF SCIENCE
by Shri Bhawani Kumar

Edition
2024

Price
₹ 450.00 (Rupees Four Hundred Fifty only)

Printed at
Narula Printers, Delhi

Preface

We find application of science in every walk of life. Science is the study of the surroundings we live in. It is a part of our day to day life. So the study of science holds great importance to all of us. It enables us to understand the world we live and the way things happen and behave.

This *Dictionary of Science* comprehensively covers terms from all branches of science, such as physics, chemistry, biology, astrology, geology, bio-chemistry and mathematics. The dictionary provides full coverage of terms, concepts and laws relating to various aspects of science. The dictionary also includes entries from other advanced areas of science, namely computers, electronics, medical, etc., incorporating the recent advances made in all these fields. Besides, it attempts to include significant number of scientists and scholars who have contributed in different fields and benefitted the humanity with their brilliance.

The dictionary has been drawn upon a large number of reliable authentic sources to ensure the quality of contents. The author has made great efforts to make the entries as concise and comprehensible as possible. The entries have been arranged alphabetically so as to make it convenient and user-friendly. The terms having more than one definitions, they have been arranged number-wise. The language of explanation has been kept at a level which an average student is expected to understand. Text has been supplemented with illustrations wherever necessary to add to the understanding of the students.

The dictionary has been designed to serve as a reference guide for students of all branches of science at higher secondary and graduate level. It attempts to provide them accurate explanations of terms, familiar or unfamiliar, that they come across in course of their studies.

The book will be of great interest to those readers as well who have not science as their specialised subject but they want to understand the concepts, laws and theories of science in various fields. With all these features the dictionary is a valuable source to all.

—Bhawani Kumar

Contents

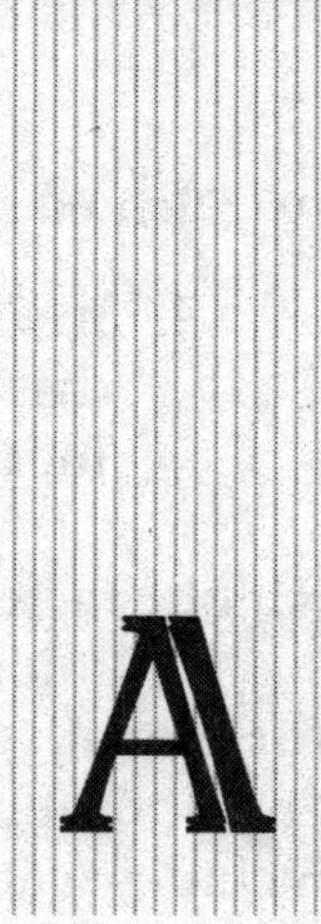

A

1. In Physics, it is a symbol for absolute temperature, ampere, angstrom and acceleration and amplitude.
2. In Chemistry, it is a symbol for absorption coefficient.
3. In Biology, it is a symbol for adenine.

Aardvark

It is a South African animal, largely found in woods and green lands. Its body is stumpy and has a long nose, tongue and ears. It eats insects.

Aardvark

Abacus

It is a frame with small balls which slide along the wire. It is used as a tool or toy for children for simple arithmetic calculations.

Abdomen

It is the posterior region of the trunk, containing the stomach and the intestines and the organ of excretion and reproduction. It is well defined in mammal.

Aberration

It is used for the following:

1. In Physics, it refers to a defect in the image formed by a lens or mirror. The defect can be corrected by an achromatic lens.

2. In Astronomy, the term is used for the apparent displacement of a star which is caused by the earth's motion around the sun.

Abiotic factor

In Biology, the term is used for non-living factors in the environment or ecosystem. It includes water, temperature, air, atmosphere, etc.

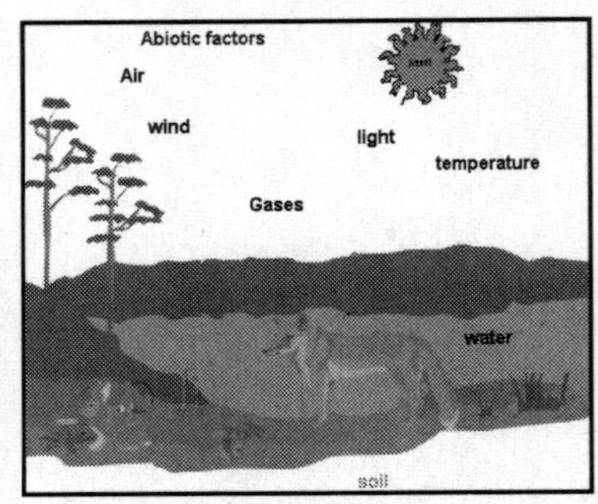

Abiotic Factor

ABO system

It is one of the major human blood group systems, based on the presence or absence of antigens on the surface of red blood cells and also of antibodies in blood serum.

Absolute time

It is the time that exists independently of any events or processes in the universe. Absolute time is a basic concept in Newton's Theory.

Absolute zero

In Physics, the lowest temperature at which the kinetic energy of molecules and atoms is minimal. It is 0 Kelvin or 273°C. It is the lowest temperature theoretically attainable.

Absorption

It refers to the following:

1. In Physics, it refers to the conversion of the energy of electromagnetic radiation, sound, etc. into other forms of energy when passed through a medium.
2. In Chemistry, it implies the taking of a gas by a solid or liquid, or taking up of a liquid by a solid.
3. In Biology, it refers to the movement of fluid or a dissolved substance across a plasma membrane. For example, in plants, water and minerals are absorbed from soils by roots, but in most of the animals, soluble food material is absorbed into cells.

Abyssal zone

It is the lower depths of the oceans, located approximately 2000 meters below, where there is no light penetration. Abyssal organisms are adapted to living in such condition.

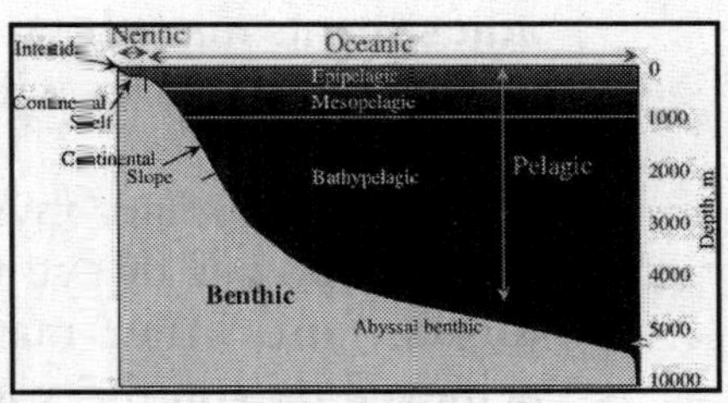

Abyssal zone

Accelerant

The term includes inflammable materials used in case of arson to start a fire. Petrol and paraffin are commonly used accelerants.

Acceleration

In Physics, it is defined as the rate of change of velocity or speed in a moving body. It is expressed as,

$$A = (v - u)/t = (v^2 - u^2)/2s$$

where t denotes the time taken, s shows the distance covered, and A represents acceleration.

Anything that causes acceleration is called accelerator.

Accelerator (symbol *a*)

It denotes the following:

1. In Physics, it is an apparatus, used for increasing kinetic energies of particles. Accelerators are widely used in research in nuclear and particle physics.
2. In Chemistry, it is the substance which increases the rate of a chemical reaction.

Access point

It is a device which serves as an important part of a wireless network. It works within its range and facilitates successful networking. It also helps in Internet networking.

Accommodation

It is used for the following:

1. In terms of animal behaviour, it refers to the

adjustments made by an animal's nervous or sensory system in accordance with the changing environmental conditions.

2. In terms of human physiology, it implies focussing. It is the power of eye to focus image on retina. In human and other mammals, accommodation is achieved by voluntary adjusting the curvature of the lens of the eye by relaxation and contraction.

Accumulator

It is a voltaic cell which can store electrical energy. It is a storage battery which can be charged and discharged. It is in automobiles.

Achilles tendon

It refers to the tendon which joins the calf muscles to the heel bone. Any damage to it may cause disability in walking.

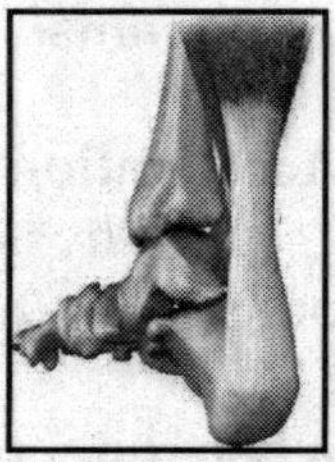

Achilles tendon

Achromatic lens

It is a lens which is used to correct chromatic aberration by combining two component lenses – one convergent and the other divergent, made of two different kinds of glasses.

Acid

It is a compound, containing hydrogen, with sour taste, which reacts with an alkali or base to produce salt and water. Acids tend to be corrosive in nature, which turn litmus red and give colour changes with other indicators.

Acid rain

It is used for shower, having a pH value of less than about 5.0, mainly caused by the oxides of sulphur and nitrogen emitted from the burning of fossil fuels. Acid rain adversely effects the flora and fauna of the region where it falls.

Acid rock

It is a form of igneous rock, predominantly consisting of

light-coloured silicate minerals (more than 65%), e.g. granite and rhyolite. Its density is low.

Acoustics

The term is used to describe the following:

1. Scientific study of sound and sound waves.
2. The characteristics of a building or theatre in terms of sound it is able to produce. In this context, no obtrusive echoes and resonances are good but the reverberation time should be near the optimum for the hall.

Acquired Immune Deficiency Syndrome (AIDS)

It is a human disease characterised by defective cell mediated immunity, caused by a retro-virus (HIV-1). A person suffering from AIDS increasingly becomes susceptible to infections. It infects and destroys T-cells which helps in combating infections. The disease is transmitted sexually or by blood or body fluids. An HIV-infected person is described as HIV-positive. The disease is incurable but anti-virus drugs can only delay the development of full blown AIDS for some years.

ACTH

Abbreviation for Adrenocorticotrophic, it is a hormone secreted by pituitary gland, which stimulates the production of cortisol, used in the treatment of arthritis.

Actinometer

It is an instrument used to measure the intensity of electromagnetic radiation. Modern actinometers are based on photoelectric effect but earlier they used fluorescence produced by the radiation on the screen or the amount of induced chemical change in suitable substance.

Actinometer

Active device

The term is used for the following:

1. An artificial satellite that receives information, amplifies that information and retransmits it.
2. An electronic component, e.g. transistor which is capable of amplification.

Active immunity

It refers to immunity acquired as a result of body's response to a foreign antigen.

Acupuncture

It is a Chinese system of treatment in which needles are used to puncture pressure points to suppress pain or cause anaesthesia.

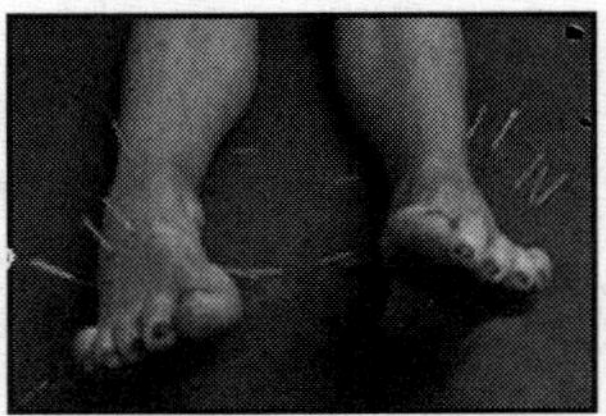

Acupuncture

Ada

Developed in the late 1970s, it is a high-level computer programming language, employed in the missile control system in the US. Now it is widely used in various other real time applications.

Adaptation

It implies the following:

1. In Physiology, it refers to the alteration in the degree of sensitivity of a sense organ to adjust with the extreme conditions normally not encountered. For example, the adjustment of the eye to very bright or dim light.
2. In the context of evolution, it denotes a change in the structure or functioning of successive generations of population to better suit the environment.

Adder

It belongs to a group of poisonous and non-poisonous snakes found all over the world, for example various species of viper, death adder of Australia, Russel's viper, etc.

Addison's disease

It is a disease which causes anaemia, low blood pressure, weakness and pigmentation of skin.

Additive

It is a substance added to another substance to improve its properties. Additives are used for a variety of purposes such as for stabilizing polymers, preventing corrosion, etc. Besides, there are food additives which are used for food preservation, for enhancing food quality and improving their texture.

Adhesion

The term refers to the following:

1. In Physics, intermolecular forces holding matter together.
2. In medical, abnormal union of inflamed parts.

Adrenal glands

The term is used for a pair of glands found very close to kidneys. They produce adrenaline and cortisol hormones in which have a wide range of effects on body. Since they are located above the kidneys, they are also called suprarenal glands.

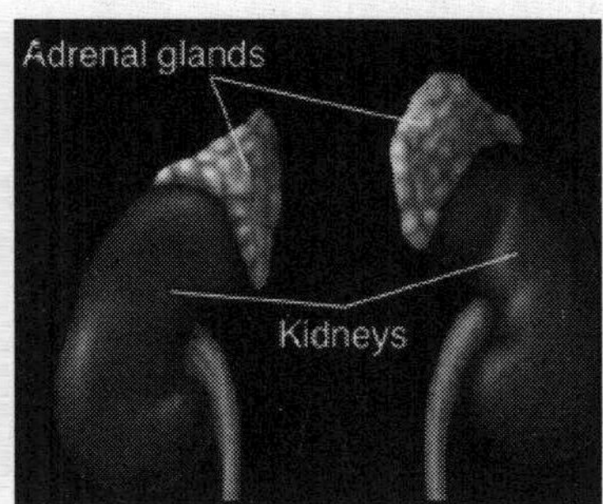

Adrenal glands

Adrenaline

It is a hormone secreted by the adrenal glands responsible for raising heartbeats, blood pressure and respiration. In fact, it prepares body for 'fight, fright and flight' at the same time it interferes with the process of digestion and excretion and stimulates the metabolism of body. It is produced when a person is excited.

Adrian, Edgar Douglas, Baron (1889-1977)

A Professor at Cambridge, he is best known as a Neurophysiologist for his work on nerve impulses. He first established that messages are conveyed by changes in the frequency of the impulses. In 1932, he was awarded Nobel Prize for Physiology or Medicine with Sir Charles Sherrington for his outstanding contribution in the field of Neurology.

Adsorbate

It is a substance absorbed on a surface.

Adsorbent

The term is used for the substance on the surface of which a substance is absorbed.

Adsorption

In Chemistry, the term is used for the accumulation of one substance on the surface of another forming a layer of gas, liquid or solid. Adsorption is a significant feature in various surface reaction such as corrosion and heterogeneous catalysis.

Adulteration

The term is widely used to refer illegal addition of any substance in food product that causes a decline in its quality. Usually, it is done to gain extra profit. It is a punishable offence.

Adventitious roots

The term refers to abnormal structures that develop on abnormal sites in unusual position in the plant body, for example, Ivy has adventitious roots on its stems.

Adventitious roots

Aerodynamics

It is a branch of physics which studies the forces exerted by air and other gases in motion with the flow of air all around the bodies moving speedily through the atmosphere. Aerodynamics also concerns with the study of motion and stability of aircraft, including the flow of gases through compressors, ducts, fans, orifices, etc.

Aerogel

It is a low density transparent material consisting of more than 90% air. Aerogels are largely used as insulators and drying agents.

Aeronautics

It refers to the study of science of travel through atmosphere, namely rocket propulsion, air navigation, aerodynamics, aircraft structures, etc.

Aeronautics

Aerosol

It refers to a colloidal dispersion of a solid or a liquid in a gas. Gradually, they are being replaced by volatile hydrocarbons because of their harmful effect on the ozone layer.

Aerospace

It includes the earth's atmosphere and the space beyond it.

Aetiology

It is the study of causation, particularly the causes of medical conditions.

Ageing

It is used to refer the decline in fitness of an organism that usually occurs with the increase in age. It is a natural process that every organism has to undergo.

Agronomy

The term is used for the scientific study of agriculture and related economy.

Air-conditioning

The term refers to the process of bringing the air to the desired level of temperature and purity. It is largely used in room and vehicles to ensure comforts.

Air pollution

Air pollution

The term is used to refer the substances released into the atmosphere that cause a wide range of harmful effects on environment. Major air pollutants are harmful and toxic gases such as carbon dioxide, carbon monoxide, sulphur dioxide, nitrogen oxides which are largely produced by vehicles and industries. Air pollution has harmful effects on human health. Carbon dioxide is a major contributor to greenhouse effect.

Air sac

It is used for the following:

1. A thin-walled structure connected to lungs in birds that increase the efficiency of respiration.
2. A structural extension to the trachea in insects which increases the surface area available for the exchange of oxygen and carbon dioxide that helps in respiration.

Albinism

The term refers to a lack of pigmentation in an organism. Albinism is a recessive hereditary disease in human beings and mammals which is caused by the absence of melanin pigment in the skin, hair, or eyes. Albinism deprives them of their natural colour.

Albumin

Albumin is a group of water soluble proteins, largely found in egg white, milk, blood and plants. It helps in the regulation of osmotic pressure.

Alcohol

The term is used for the organic compounds with -OH group. Alcohols are of different types depending on their chemical reaction. They react with acids to give esters and dehydration to give alkenes or ethers. Alcohols are used as drink, as solvent in paints and resins.

Algae

It belongs to a large group of aquatic plants which contain chlorophylls and other pigments. Algae may be unicellular and multicellular.

Alimentary canal

It is a tubular organ, divided into a series of sections, namely mouth, oesophagus and intestine each section being involved in different activities of food processing, for example, ingestion digestion, absorption, elimination etc. of food. In most animals, there are two openings in it but in some animals there is only one opening, e.g. hydra and jellyfish.

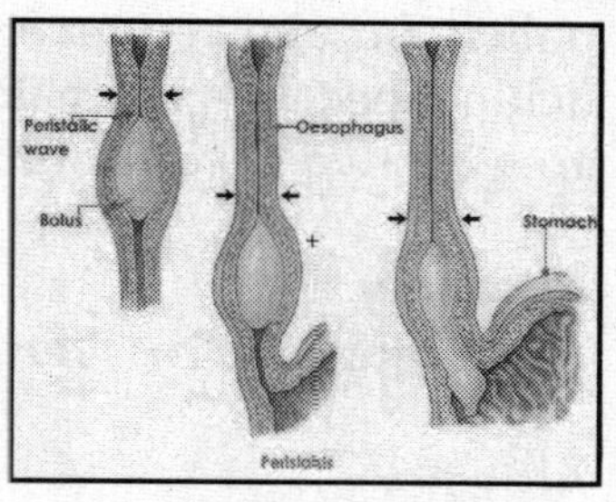

Alimentary canal

Alkali

It belongs to bases that is soluble in water and give hydroxide ions, for example—sodium hydroxide.

Alkali metals

These are the metals found in the first group of the periodic table. Alkali metals are lithium, potassium, sodium, caesium, rubidium, and francium. They react with water to produce alkalis.

Alkaloid

Alkaloids are basic organic compounds that contain nitrogen atoms. They are largely derived from plants and have pronounced pharmacological properties. However, some of the alkaloids are toxic but they are used as analgesics. Alkaloids are classified into various groups, namely the pyridine group, the indole group, the quinoline group, the tropine group, the isoquinoline group, etc.

Allele

It is one of the alternative forms of genes. Usually, there are two alleles of any one gene, one from the father and the other from the mother, but there may be many alleles of a gene. Each of the allele has a unique nucleotide sequence.

Allergy

It refers to a condition in the body which is characterised by abnormal immune response to certain antigens such as dust, pollen, fur and certain food and drugs. Its symptoms include itching, oedema, dermatosis, high fever, etc. Anti-hestamines are effective to control the allergy.

Allogamy

It refers to cross fertilization in plants.

Alligator

It is a large reptile belonging to crocodile family. Alligators are almost like crocodiles except that they have broader, flatter heads with round snouts.

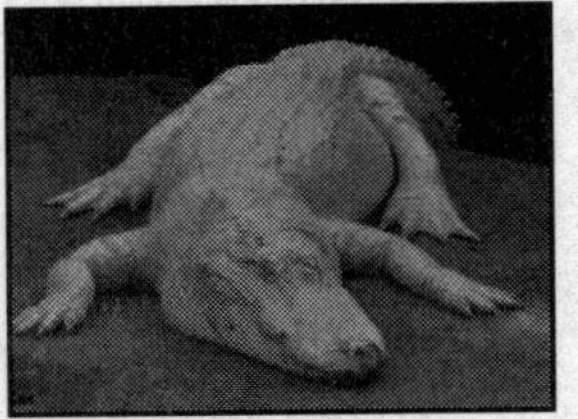

Alligator

Allopathy

It refers to a highly advanced system of treatment of disease based on English medicine.

Allotrope

It represents element found in more than one natural form – solid, liquid or gaseous – without any change in chemical form. Graphite and diamond are allotropes of carbon. Sulphur has four allotropes.

Alloy

The term is used for a substance consisting of two metals or a metal and a non-metal, e.g. brass is an alloy of copper and tin while steel is an alloy of iron and carbon.

Alluvial deposits

The term refers to sediments deposited in a river bed, ranging from particles to coarse gravels.

Alpha centauri

Used in astrology, the term refers to the biggest star in the constellation Centaurus, while the faintest star is called Proxima centauri, which is nearest to the sun.

Alpha decay

It denotes radioactive disintegration, leading to emission of alpha particles.

Alternating current

It is an electric current that flows for an interval of time in one direction and then reverses its direction. Electrical energy is produced as alternating current in power stations. Alternating current is continuously varying and is different from direct current.

Altimeter

It is a device used for measuring height above sea level. It is used in aircraft. It consists of an aneroid barometer.

Altimeter

Altitude

The term refers to the height of an object or point relative to sea level or ground level. It is expressed as an angle.

ALU

Abbreviation for Arithmetic Logic Unit, it refers to the part of the Central Processing Unit of a computer where binary data is acted upon with mathematical operations, e.g. addition, subtraction, multiplication, division, etc. ALU can even negate a number.

Aluminium (*Symbol* Al)

It is a lustrous white metallic element, belonging to group 3 of the periodic table, atomic number 13, atomic weight 26.28, melting point 660.45°, boiling point 2520°C. The metal is highly reactive, it has many compounds and has so many uses. The metal is extracted from bauxite. Pure aluminium is soft and ductile, however, its strength can be increased by work hardening. It is light, corrosion resistant and has good electrical conductivity that makes it highly useful. In terms of weight, aluminium is the third most abundantly found element in the earth's crust (8.1%).

Aluminosilicate

It is a rock-forming mineral in some clays, mica, zeolite, feldspar, etc. Besides, it is widely used in cement, china glass, etc.

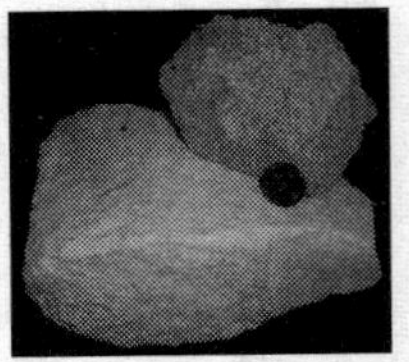
Aluminosilicate

Alums

It is a group of double salt, used for salt of aluminium metal with another metal or double salt of aluminium and potassium. The alums are isomorphous.

Alvarez, Luis Walter (1911-88)

He was a US Physicist who was awarded the Nobel Prize for his contribution in the field of physics. He made the first large bubble chamber in 1959 and also developed the techniques for using it to study charged particles. During World War II, he worked on the radar and the atomic bomb.

Alveolus

It implies the following:

1. It is used for tiny air sacs found in the lungs of the mammals and reptiles at the end of each bronchiole. It is supplied with many minute blood capillaries and is also the site where exchange of gases takes place.
2. The socket in the jawbone where the tooth is rooted.

Alzheimer's disease

It is a neurological disorder characterised by shrinkage of the brain tissues and changes in the neurotransmitter system in the brain. It is manifested as a progressive loss in the intellectual ability. Generally, this occurs in advance stage of life. It is an impairment of higher mental faculties.

Amalgam

It is an alloy of mercury containing one or more metals except iron and platinum, which may be liquid or solid.

Amber

Amber

It is yellow or reddish-brown fossil resin, used in jewellery and ornaments. It is found in rock strata throughout the world and has the property of acquiring electrical charge when rubbed.

Amenorrhea

It refers to a condition in which menstruation is absent in human being. Amenorrhea can be primary or secondary. It is primary when menstruation has not started at all, but when it is absent after it has started, it is called secondary amenorrhea. Primary may be due to some congenital defects like Turner's syndrome, but secondary may be due to factors such as diabetes, depression or hormonal disorders.

Americium (*Symbol* Am)

It is a radioactive metallic element belonging to the actinides, melting point being 994±4°C; boiling point 2607°C. It was discovered by G.T. Seaborg, and produced by bombarding uranium 238 with alpha particles.

Ames test

The test is used to study the effects of a chemical on the rate of growth of bacterial cells. In this test, special strains of bacteria are used to evaluate the effects of chemicals. It is widely used in screening chemicals present in the environment to determine the possible carcinogenic activity.

Amino acids

The term is used for a group of water-soluble organic compound, represented by the general formula $R\text{-}CH(NH_2)COOH$. The compounds are formed by replacing a hydrogen atom in a hydrocarbon radical by amino group.

Proteins consist of 20 commonly occurring amino acids. Some amino acids are essential for general well-being of humans.

Ammeter

It is an instrument used for measuring current in electric circuit. Mainly, there are three type of ammeter – moving-coil ammeter, thermoammeter and moving-iron ammeter.

Ammeter

Ammonia (NH_3)

It is a colourless, highly soluble in water and alcohol, with a strong pungent smell. It is widely used in refrigeration, explosives, dyestuffs, resins and in the manufacturing of nitrogen fertilizers.

Amnesia

It refers to a condition which is characterised by partial or total loss of memory due to pathological reasons.

Amniocentesis

The term refers to the process in which amniotic fluid is taken out from a pregnant woman to determine the condition of the foetus. It is done by putting a hollow needle through the abdomen wall of the pregnant woman and fluid from the uterus is drawn off. Usually, it is done to detect sex and hereditary disease.

Amoeba

Formerly placed in the phylum Rhizopoda, it is a genus of protists now classified as amoebozoans, amoeba have temporary body projections that help it in locomotion and feeding as a result it has a constantly changing body shape. Most species live freely in mud, soil, or water but a few are parasitic.

Ampere (*Symbol* A)

It refers to the rate of flow of current in a circuit. It is the SI unit of electric current. One ampere is equal to 6.28×10^{18}

electrons per second or a flow of charge of one coulomb per second.

Ampère, Andrè Marie (1775-1836)

He was a French Physicist who formulated Ampere's Law. The SI unit of electrical current Ampere is named after him. He is widely known for putting electromagnetism on a mathematical basis.

Amphetamines

It is a drug which stimulates the central nervous system, suppresses appetite, inhibits sleep and effects mood. Its side effects are harmful to the health.

Amphibia

It represents the class of vertebrates which live both on land and in water and breath through skin and lungs. Frogs, toads, newts and salamanders belong to this group. They have smooth moist skin and has gills when young which develops into lungs when they grow older.

Amplifier

It is an electronic device which increases the strength of an electric signal by drawing power from a source other than the input signal.

Amplifier

Amplitude

It refers to the measurement of the distance from the highest to the lowest excursion of motion. It is the maximum displacement of an oscillation from its equilibrium position.

Amputation

The term refers to surgical removal of a limb because of disease, infection or injury.

Anaconda

It is non-poisonous snake, growing up to 9 meters, largely

found in South America. It kills its prey by coiling around them tightly thus causing them to suffocate to death. It then swallows its prey. It does not lay eggs but give birth to its young ones. Its skin is olive green with rings or spots on it. It is the largest snake in the world.

Anaemia

It refers to a medical condition characterised by deficiency of haemoglobin in blood caused by lack of red blood cells. It symptoms include weakness, fatigue, breathlessness, etc. It can be cured by the intake of iron and vitamin B_{12}.

Analgesic

It is a substance that helps reducing pain without causing unconsciousness. Analgesic drugs are of different categories such as morphine and its derivatives, non-steroidal anti-inflammatory drugs, local anaesthesia, etc.

Analog computer

It is a device used for solving problems by measuring one quantity in terms of another but it is not as accurate as digital computers.

Analog computer

Anaphylaxis

It is a medical condition in which body reacts extremely to something when eaten or touched. It occurs because of the release of histamine and other substances. It can be manifested as a localised reaction or generalised one with severe symptoms like difficulty in breathing, unconsciousness, drop in blood pressure sometimes leading to even heart failure and death.

Anatomy

The term refers to the study of the internal structure of living organisms by dissection and microscopic examination. It constitutes an integral part of the medicine.

Androgen

It belongs to one of the group of male hormones which is responsible for the development of sexual organs and secondary sexual characters.

Anemometer

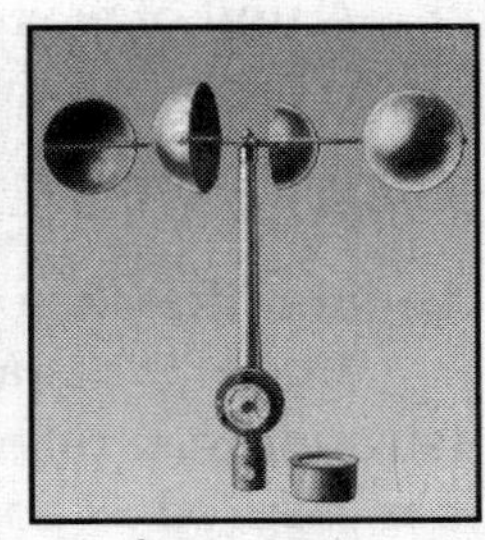
Anemometer

It is an instrument used for measuring the speed and direction of wind and other flowing fluid. The instrument is calibrated to give a wind speed. A simple vane anemometer has many cups or blades attached to a central spindle which rotates with the flow of wind or fluid while a hot-wire anemometer has an electrically heated wire which is cooled when the fluid passing round it flows. The temperature and resistance of the wire depend on the flow of fluid.

Angina pectoris

It is a medical condition in which a person feels severe pain in the chest radiating to the arm, with suffocation caused by inadequate supply of blood to the cardiac muscles.

Angiocardiography

It is a technique for the radiographic examination of the blockage in the arteries, heart chambers and thoracic veins. A radiocontrast agent, typically containing iodine, is injected into the blood vessels and X-rays are used to examine the tissues.

Angiology

It refers to the science of blood and lymph vessels.

Angioplasty

It is a medical procedure used for mechanical repair of damaged blood vessels, in which an empty and collapsed balloon, on a guided wire, is passed into the blocked blood vessel and then inflated to fixed size using water pressures to some 75 to 500 times the normal blood pressure that crushes the fatty deposits and open up the blood vessel thus improving the flow of blood. The balloon is then deflated and withdrawn.

Angstrom (*Symbol* Å)

A unit of wavelength and electromagnetic radiation, it has been replaced by the nanometer. Named after Anders Angstrom, one Å = 0.1 nanometer.

Angular distance

Angular distance is a way to express sizes or distances in astronomy. It refers to the distance between two objects which is measured as angles on the celestial spheres. It is expressed in degrees, arc-minutes or arc-seconds.

Anhydrous

It refers to a chemical compound which lacks water, however, particularly applied to salt lacking their water crystallisation.

Animal

The term is used for any member of Animalia kingdom which includes multicellular organisms which develop from embryos. These organisms largely depend on other organisms or organic matter. Animals have evolved specialised sense organs to adjust with the changes of the environment and they are typically mobile.

Animal

Animal cell

It is the basic unit of animal body which has cell membrane, cytoplasm, nucleus, etc. The structure of animal cell is different from that of the plant cell.

Anisogamy

It refers to sexual reproduction that involves the fusion of gametes which may have difference in size and form also.

Annual

The term is used for a plant which has a complete life cycle of one year. It is during this period that the plant germinates, blooms, produces seeds and dies, for example sunflower.

Annual ring

The term is used for the rings formed in the stems or roots of dicots every year from which the age of the plant is calculated. This ring is caused by the secondary thickening of the stems or roots. Two such rings are formed every year.

Anode

It refers to positive electrodes through which current enters.

Antacids

The term represents the medicine which corrects or nullifies acidity particularly in the stomach.

Anteater

It is an animal which has long snout and whip-like tongue which helps it to catch ants, termites and insects. It is a nocturnal animal and has burrowing habits, however, it can climb trees also.

Antenna

It refers to the following:

1. In physics, it is device used for sending radio waves into the atmosphere and also for receiving them
2. In zoology, it is that sensitive organ of the insects, located mainly in the head, which picks up sensations.

Antenna

Anther

The term is used for the upper part of a plant stamen which has two lobes, each of them contains two sacs in which there are numerous pollen grains. These pollens get released when the anther ruptures. The anther is usually yellow in colour.

Anthrax

It is a serious disease of animal which is caused by *Bacillus anthracis*.

Antibiotics

The term refers to chemical substances, obtained from bacteria or fungi or synthesised, and can destroy or inhibit the growth of harmful bacteria. Antibiotics are used to treat various infections but they also affect the body's natural defence mechanism. Penicillins, streptomycin, the tetracyclines are the examples of antibiotics.

Antibody

It is a protein produced by the body in the blood by white blood corpuscles or lymphocytes in response to entry of some foreign substances to destroy toxins or antigens from bacteria. Antibody production is an important aspect of immune response.

Anticoagulant

It refers to a substance which prevents the formation of blood clots. Some medicine such as heparin, aspirin, and warfrain are anticoagulants used to treat heart attacks and thrombosis.

Antifreeze

It is a substance usually added to water in the cooling systems, e.g. internal combustion engine, to lower its freezing point so that it does not solidify at below zero temperature. Ethane-1,2-diol (ethyl glycol) is an example of antifreeze.

Antigen

It refers to any foreign body or protein which initiates immune response in the body. It is a substance that evokes the production of antibodies. Antigens may be formed in, or introduced into, the body.

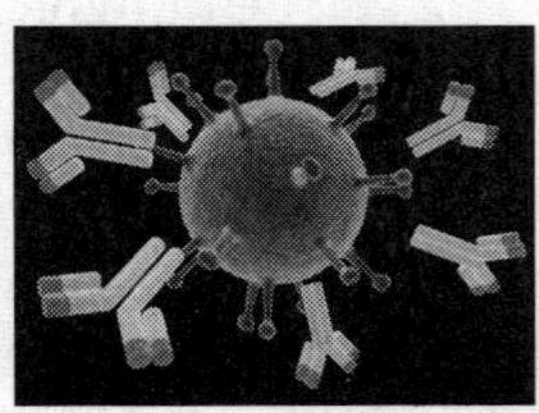

Antigen

Antihistamine

It is a substance which propels the action of histamines in the body. It is used to reduce or prevent allergic reactions in the body, e.g. hay fever. Antihistamines are used to prevent motion sickness and induce sleep since its side effects cause sleepiness.

Antimony (*Symbol Sb*)

It is a silvery white metallic element belonging to group 15 (formerly VB) of the periodic table, widely used in alloying agent. Antimony is extracted from stibnite (Sb_2S_3).

Antioxidants

Antioxidants are substances that inhibit or delay the process of oxidation. It protects the cells from the damage caused by free radicals. Antioxidants have wider uses such as preservatives in foodstuff and cosmetics and to prevent the degradation of rubber and gasoline.

Antioxidants

Antipyretic

It presents the drugs used to calm down fever by decreasing the body temperature. Some analgesics, for example, aspirin, paracetamol have antipyretic properties.

Antiseptic

It is a substance that inhibits the growth and development of microorganisms. It is non-toxic to the cells of the body. Carbolic acid is a common antiseptic, others being hydrogen peroxide and ethanol. Antiseptics are used to treat minor wounds.

Antivenin

Antivenin is a sterile, non-pyrogenic preparation used in the treatment of snake bites or venomous bites or stings. It neutralises the venom if given at the earliest thus halting further damage but does not reverse damage already done. The principle of antivenin is based on that of the vaccine.

Anus

It is the terminal opening at the opposite end of most of the animals' digestive tract from the mouth, through which waste material is expelled.

Aorta

It is a major blood vessel in the higher vertebrates which is branched into many smaller arteries. It is through aorta that the oxygenated blood leaves the heart from the left ventricles. The aorta with its lots of branches is responsible for the supply of oxygen and other nutrients to all living cells of the body.

Apes

Apes belong to the Pongidae family which have no tails. There are four kinds of apes, chimpanzee, gorilla, gibbon and orang-utan. They are largely found in east and southeast Asia. Of all these apes, chimpanzee is very close to mankind.

Apes

Aperture

It is an opening that allows light to fall onto an instrument's optics. It is the effective diameter of a lens. The light-gathering power of a telescope is closely related to the square of the aperture.

Aphelion

It is the point on a planet's elliptical orbit at which it is farthest from the sun. The earth is at aphelion on or about 4 July when it is at a distance of 1.0167 astronomical units from the sun.

Aphrodisiac

The term includes drugs or food which is said to have properties that stimulate sexual excitement.

Apogee

It is the point in the orbit of the moon, or an artificial satellite at which it is furthest from the earth. At apogee the moon is at a distance of 406700 km from the earth.

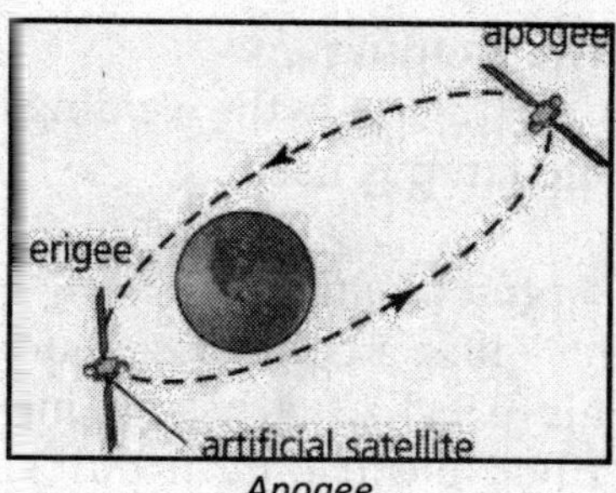

Apogee

Aqua regia

It is a mixture of concentrated nitric acid and concentrated hydrochloric acid in the ratio 1:3 respectively. It is a powerful oxidising agent which dissolves all metals including gold and platinum except silver.

Aqueous humour

It is the fluid that fills the space between the cornea and the lens of the eye in the vertebrates. It serves as a source of supply of nutrients to the cornea and the lens. It also maintains the shape of the eye.

Archaeology

It refers to the study of cultures, human antiquities and human life of the past based on the buildings and remains found in the ground.

Archimedes' principle

The principle states that the weight of the liquid displaced by a floating body is equal to the weight of the body. The principle is also stated that when a body is partially or fully immersed6 in a fluid, the upthrust on the body is equal to the weight of the fluid displaced. The principle is named after its discoverer, the Greek mathematician Archimedes.

Arachnida

The term represents the class of terrestrial arthropods including ticks, mites, spiders, scorpions, etc. An arachnid's body is divided into an anterior cephalothorax and a posterior abdomen. Some arachnids like ticks and mites are parasitic but most of them are free-living.

Arc welding

It refers to the welding of metals in which high temperature arc lamp is used.

Argon (*Symbol* Ar)

It is a colourless, odourless rare noble gas found in the air (0.93%). It is used in inert atmospheres in welding and gas-filled electric-light bulbs. The gas was identified by Lord Rayleigh and Sir William Ramsey.

Armadillo

It belongs to the order Edenta and includes sloth armadillos and anteaters. They are nocturnal and are largely found in South America. They feed on insects. Their body is covered with long scales arranged in rings.

Armadillo

Armature

It refers to any moving part in an electrical machine, e.g. the coil of a dynamo or an electric motor, in which voltage is induced by a magnetic field.

Arsenic (Symbol *As*)

It is a metalloid element of group XV in the periodic table, its atomic number 33; atomic weight 74.9; melting point 817° C, sublimes at 613° C. It has three isotopes – yellow, grey and black; the grey one is the most stable and most common. Arsenic is used in insecticides and in semiconductors. Its small doses are useful as medicine but its high dose is poisonous.

Artery

It refers to a blood vessel which has muscular walls that carries blood from the heart towards the various body organs. Accumulation of fatty deposits in its walls results in heart problems eventually blocking the blood flow.

Arthropod

Arthropod

It represents an invertebrate animal whose body consists of segments, e.g. head, thorax and abdomen. Their body is covered with a layer – cuticle, which acts as a protective exoskeleton. Arthropods have over one million species inhabiting marine, freshwater and terrestrial habitats.

Arthritis

It is a disease affecting old age with symptoms like swelling and stiffness of the joints. There are of different types of arthritis such as rheumatoid arthritis, osteoarthritis, juvenile arthritis and ankylosing spondilitis. Analgesic and anti-inflammatory drugs are helpful.

Artificial insemination

It is an artificial method of conception in which semen is deposited at the mouth of the uterus with the help of syringe to make conception. It is done at a time when ovulation is most likely in the female. In humans, it is done in case of infertility or impotence, while in animals, it is done for selective breeding.

Artificial intelligence

It is a subfield of computer science concerned with the programs which when performed require intelligence such as playing computer game, interpreting images and reasoning and understanding languages.

Asbestos

The term belongs to a group of fibrous amphibole minerals which has wide commercial uses because of its resistance to heat, high electrical resistance and chemical inertness. Canada is the largest producer of asbestos in the world, followed by Russia, South Africa, Zimbabwe and China.

Ascorbic acid

It refers to vitamin C largely found in fruit. It is soluble in water. Ascorbic acid is necessary for the growth of healthy tissue. Its deficiency causes scurvy disease.

Asexual

It refers to reproduction in which new individuals are produced without the formation of gametes. In asexual reproduction, both parents are not involved. It largely occurs in plants and microorganisms.

Asthenosphere

The term is used for the earth's mantle that extends to a depth of about 250 km where rocks are solid. It is said that it is a zone of partial melting.

Asthma

It is a respiratory problem in which a person feels difficulty in breathing which is caused by the constriction of bronchial pipe. It is because of allergy or hereditary dispositions.

Aston Francis William (1877-1945)

He was a British Chemist and Physicist who is credited to have designed the mass spectrograph that helped him in the discovery of isotopes of neon, and was thus able to explain non-integral atomic weights. He was awarded the Nobel Prize for Chemistry in 1922.

Aston Francis William

Astrology

It deals with the study of the positions of the stars and the movements of the planets in the context of the belief that they influence human life which is based on the position of these bodies at the time of birth of the individual.

Astrometry

It is the branch of Astronomy which deals with the measurement of positions, movement and the size of the celestial bodies on the celestial sphere.

Astronomical unit

The term denotes the mean distance between the sun and the earth which is equal to 149597870 km.

Astronomy

It refers to the study of space and the heavenly bodies. It includes the study of the universe, its origin and evolution, cosmology, astrophysics and celestial mechanics.

Astronomy

Astrophysics

It relates to the scientific study of the physical and chemical structures and evolution of the stars, galaxies and planets, etc, including the generation and transportation of energy within stars, dynamics of stars.

Atmosphere (*Symbol* atm)

The term is used for the following:

1. The gaseous envelop that surrounds the earth. It consists of nitrogen (78.085%), oxygen (29.95%), argon (0.93%), carbon dioxide (0.03%), neon (0.0018%), helium (0.0005%), krypton (0.0001%) and xenon (0.00001%), besides water vapour and dust particles.
2. A unit of pressure equal to 101325 Pascal. Atmospheric pressure is equal to 760.0 mmHg.

Atoll

Largely found in the Pacific Oceans, it refers to a circular coral reef surrounding a shallow central lagoon. Its size ranges from a few kilometres to more than 100 km across. It may be continuous or broken into small islets.

Atom

It refers to the smallest unit of matter, consisting of nucleus protons, neutrons and electrons. The electrons have negative charge, protons have positive charge and neutrons are neutral.

Atomic bomb

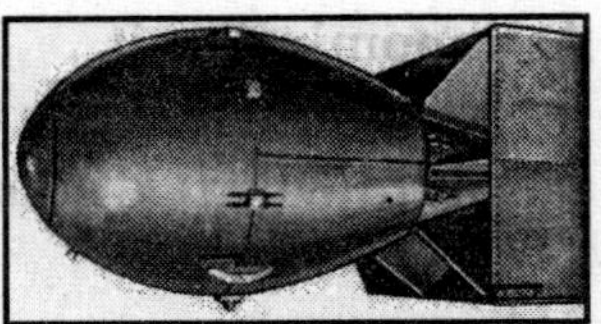
Atomic bomb

The term is used for the explosives based on the principle of nuclear fission. The nuclear fission of one uranium atom yields about 3.2×10^{-11} joule whereas 6.4×10^{-19} joule can be obtained from the combustion of one carbon atom. When the nuclei of uranium-238 and plutonium-239 are bombarded with neutrons, it produces tremendous amount of energy within fraction of seconds. The same principle is followed in the nuclear reactors.

Atomic clock

It is an apparatus used for measuring time. It is also used for standardising time. Atomic clock is based on periodic phenomena within atoms or molecules.

Atomic energy

The form of energy produced as a result of nuclear fission or nuclear fusion. This is based on Einstein's formula of $E = mc^2$. This is used in nuclear power station to generate electricity. It has many uses.

Atomic number (*Symbol Z*)

It represents the number of protons in the nucleus of an atom which is equal to the number of electrons orbiting the nucleus in a neutral atom. It is also called proton number.

Atomic pile

The term is used to refer the early form of nuclear reactor in which graphite was used as a moderator.

Atomic volume

It is defined as the relative atomic mass of an element divided by its density.

Atrophy

It is used for the degeneration of an organ or part of the body which could be in terms of size or function or both.

Atropine

It is a poisonous alkaloid extracted from plants and is used in medicine to treat various diseases such as colic, to reduce secretions, etc.

Attenuation

The term is used for the following:

1. In Medical, the fall of disease-producing ability of a microorganism that can be achieved by chemical treatment, drying, heating or irradiation. Attenuated bacteria or viruses are used for immunisation.
2. In Physics, the loss of intensity of sound, radiation, etc. when it passes through a medium. It can happen because of scattering or absorption.
3. In brewing and wine and spirit production, it refers to the conversion of carbohydrates in alcohol by yeasts.

Audibility

It represents the perceptibility of hearing which is affected with the increase in age. The audibility limits of the human ear range between 20 hertz and 20,000 hertz, 20 being the low sound and 20,000 the shrill whistle.

Audiofrequency

It is the frequency which a human ear is able to catch.

Audiometer

It is an instrument used to measure the hearing capacity of human ear with the help of sound of known frequency and intensity generated by the instrument.

Audiometer

Audio nerve

It refers to eight cranial nerves that transmit sensory information from the ear to the brain. It is also important for controlling hearing and balance.

Autism

It represents a mental condition in which a person particularly children are unable to communicate by speech or have normal relationships with others. One in every 10,000 children may suffer from autism. It is more frequent in boys than girls. A person suffering from autism is resistant to change of any kind.

Autoimmunity

It is a condition characterised by an abnormal immune response to a person's own antigen, for example, rheumatoid arthritis and multiple sclerosis. It occurs because the T-cells fail to recognise the various antigens.

Autosome

It refers to chromosomes other than the sex chromosomes in a cell.

Auxanometer

The term is used for mechanical instruments used to study the movement or growth of plant organs. There is a recording device in auxanometer that translates the increase in stem height into the movement of needle in the scale.

Auxin

It represents a group of plant hormones responsible for growth, initiation of root formation in cuttings and maintenance of apical dominance.

Aves

It represents the group of invertebrates which evolved from reptiles in the Jurassic period. Their forelimbs are modified into wings, their skeleton is light and many of the bones have struts to provide strength and air sacs to provide extra oxygen in flight. Their skin is loose and has no sweat glands which help in sustaining body temperature.

Aves

Axis

The term is used differently in different contexts as follows:

1. In Mathematics, a line in symmetry with a figure, curve or a body or about which it rotates. Also used for one of a set of reference lines used to locate points on a graph or in a coordinate system.
2. In Anatomy, the second cervical vertebra, which articulates with the atlas.

Axon

It is a long thread-like extension of a nerve cell carrying the nerve impulse away from the cell body to the nerve cells or muscles.

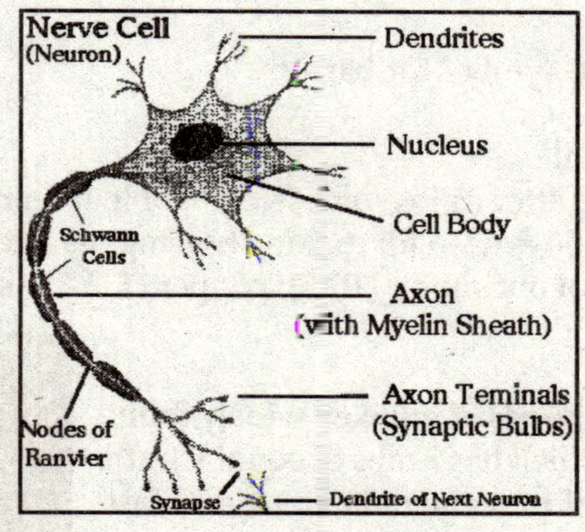

Axon

Azurite

It refers to a deep blue secondary mineral, usually formed in the upper zone of copper ore deposits. It is, in fact, a hydrated basic carbonate of copper used as a gemstone.

❑

B

B

It is used differently in different context as follows:

1. In Physics, the symbol of susceptance. Also the symbol for magnetic flux density.
2. In Chemistry, the symbol for boron.

Ba

It is the symbol for barium.

Babbit metal

Named after its inventor Isaac Babbit, it represents a group of related alloys used for making bearings as it reduces friction. It consists of antimony (10%), copper (1-2%) and lead.

Baboons

It is a species of monkey widely found in Africa which has limbs of equal length. Its power of movement is quick and fast.

Baboons

Bacillus

It refers to rod-shaped bacterium, ubiquitous in soil and air, responsible for many diseases in animals and man. Anthrax in animals and tuberculosis in human are caused by bacillus.

Back cross

The term is used for a mating between individuals to identify the hidden recessive alleles. This helps to find out the genetic make-up of an individual.

Background radiation

The term is used to refer the ionizing radiation present on the surface of the earth and in the atmosphere. Its intensity is low and is caused by the cosmic rays and by the presence of radio isotopes in the rocks, soil and atmosphere.

Backup

It refers to a resource that can be used as a substitute to a system in case of failure or loss of data from a computer file. It is, in fact, a copy of the original saved to be used in case the original is destroyed or data is lost or tampered due to any reason.

Bacteria

It represents to a group of microorganism, found everywhere, which is single-celled and has a cell wall of unique composition. A bacteria cell can be spiral, spherical, rod-shaped, corkscrew-shaped, comma-shaped. The bacteria range in size from 0.5 to 5 µm. In majority of bacteria reproduction is asexual, by simple division of cells. Bacteria play a significant role in the decay and decomposition of organic material.

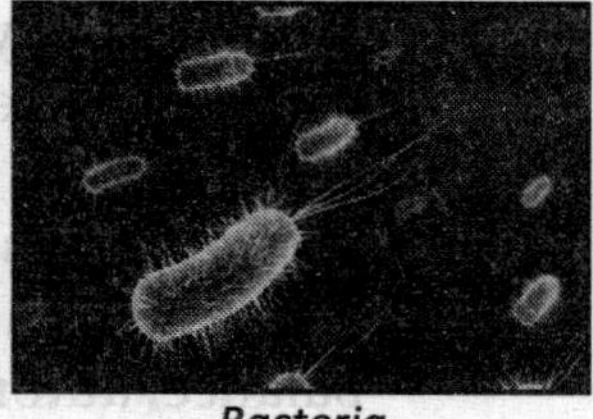

Bacteria

Bactericidal

It refers to a substance which has capability to kill bacteria. Common bactericidal includes antibiotics, disinfectants and antiseptics.

Bacteriology

It is the scientific study of bacteria particularly disease-causing bacteria (in men and cattle). It includes its form, function, classification and reproduction.

Bacteriophage

It refers to a virus attack of a bacterium in which the virus alters the general structure of it by integrating its DNA. The virus becomes parasitic within the bacteria and changes the genetic make-up of them. It is because of these characteristics that they hold importance in genetic engineering.

Baking soda ($NaHCO_3$)

It is sodium bicarbonate which reacts with acids to give carbon dioxide. It is a white crystalline solid soluble in water, and slightly soluble in ethanol. It is widely used in the treatment of acid spillage and also used as an antacids besides, in textiles, fire extinguishers, tanning, paper, etc.

Balance

The term is used differently in different context to mean the following:

1. In animal physiology, equilibrium in the posture of body. In vertebrates, it is maintained by an organ in the inner ear.
2. An apparatus used for accurate weigh. It is different types such as simple beam balance, substitution balance, automatic electronic balance, etc.
3. In terms of diet, it is used to denote a diet that includes all necessary nutrients, e.g. carbohydrates, protein, minerals, fats, salts and vitamins in right proportion required for the proper growth and development of body and maintenance of good health.

Baleen

It is used for the plates in the upper jaw of toothless which acts as a sieve in separating food particles, e.g. plankton, on which the whales feed.

Ballistic pendulum

It is a device used for measuring the velocity of a projectile, e.g. bullet. It works on the principle of the laws of conservation of linear momentum and of energy.

Ballistic pendulum

Ballistic missile

It refers to a missile that follows the sub-orbital ballistic flight path to deliver one or more warheads to a predetermined target. A ballistic missile can be fired from fixed sites or mobile launchers including vehicles and aircraft, ships and submarines.

Ballistics

It refers to the study of the motion and impact of projectiles, particularly those which follow a parabolic flight path on the surface of the earth.

Bandwidth

It is the frequency range over which a radio signal spreads but the signal is of specified frequency.

Bar

It is a unit of pressure in the CGS system which is equal to 10^6 dynes per square centimetre, or 10^5 pascals or 10^5 newtons per square meter.

Bar code

It is a code consisting of thick and thin parallel lines which contain computer readable information about the product such as price.

Bar code

Barbiturates

It refers to a group of drugs derived from barbituric acid, which acts as a sedative on the central nervous system. Earlier it was used in sleeping pills but now its use is limited due to its toxic side effects.

Barium (*Symbol* Ba)

It is a silvery white element belonging to group 2 (formally II) of the periodic table, its boiling point 1640°C and melting point 725°C. It is used as getter in vacuum system. Barium sulphate is used as barium meal in the X-ray of alimentary canal. It was identified by Karl Scheele and extracted by Humphrey Davy in 1808.

Bark

It is mostly the dead cell, which acts as the protective layer of the woody stems and cells.

Barn

It presents the unit of area equal to 10^{-28} square meter. Often it is used for measuring cross sections in nuclear interactions involving incident particles.

Barograph

It is an instrument used in meteorology for recording variations in atmospheric pressure over a period of time. The variations are recorded on paper. It has an aneroid barometer.

Barometer

It is an instrument that measures atmospheric pressure. It is mainly of two type – the mercury barometer and the aneroid barometer. The mercury barometer is the simplest and more accurate than the aneroid barometer but the aneroid barometer is much more convenient and robust.

Barometer

Barrel

It is a measurement of volume equal to 35 UK gallon which is approximately equal to 159 litres. It is widely used in chemical industry.

Barye

It is a CGS unit of pressure equal to 0.1 pascal (one dyne per square centimeter).

Barytes

It is the chief ore of barium, usually white in colour but may also be yellow, grey, or brown. It is an orthorhombic form of barium sulphate. It is largely found in Spain, the USA and the Andalusia.

Basal metabolic rate

It is the required rate of energy metabolism to maintain an animal while it is at rest. It is defined in terms of heat produced per unit time. It is expressed in kilojoules of heat released per square meter of body surface per hour ($kJm^{-2}h^{-1}$). It reflects the energy consumed for different functions such as heartbeat, transportation, nervous activity and secretion. The BMR varies organ to organ, for example, the BMR of brain tissue is greater than the skin tissue. The BMR is proportional to body weight.

Basalt

It is the igneous rock, mainly composed of calcium-rich plagioclase feldspar and pyroxene. It is fine-grained and is black in colour. It is the commonest type of lava.

Base meta

The term is commonly used for relatively cheap metal such as iron and lead, which on being exposed to air, heat, or moisture oxidises, corrodes or tarnishes, compared to expensive metal like gold and silver.

Battery

It refers to a number of secondary or primary electric cells, connected together in series or parallel. A common car battery or accumulator consists of six secondary cells, connected in series, while a torch battery is usually a dry cell.

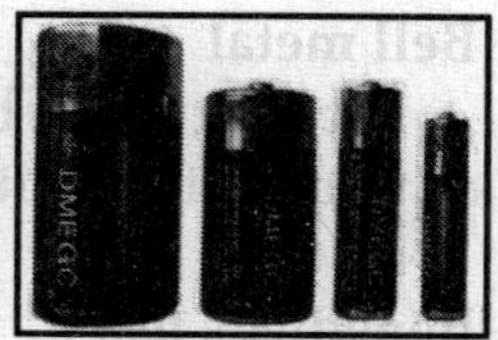
Battery

Bauxite

It is the chief ore of aluminium. It is clay-like and amorphous mainly formed by the weathering of rocks. It is the main source of aluminium. Australia, Guinea, Jamaica, Russia, Brazil are the producers of aluminium in the world.

BCG vaccine

Abbreviated form of Bacille Calmette-Guerian vaccine, it contains a strain of attenuated tubercle bacillus, which acts as an antigen. Named after its discoverer Calmette and Guerian, it is used to vaccinate against tuberculosis.

BCG vaccine

BCS theory

Developed by Nobel laureates John Bardeen, Leon Cooper and Robert Schrieffer, the theory explains superconductivity. It is the first microscopic theory of superconductivity. The theory is also used in nuclear physics to describe the pairing interaction between nucleons in an atomic nucleus.

Beckmann thermometer

It is a thermometer used for measuring the small changes in temperature, particularly for measuring the depression of freezing point or elevation of boiling point of liquids, when solute is added.

Becquerel (*Symbol* Bq)

Named after the French Scientist Henry Becquerel who discovered radioactivity in 1896, it is the SI unit of radioactivity.

Bell metal

It is a type of bronze, consisting of 60-85% copper, alloyed with tin, often with zinc, used in casting bells.

Benedict's test

It is a biochemical test, done to detect sugar level in solutions. The Benedict's reagent is used in the test as the copper sulphate in Benedict's solution reacts with reducing sugars. A red colour shows high concentration of sugar, yellow denotes lower sugar level and green indicates the absence of sugar.

Benthos

The term is used for the plants and animals found at the bottom of the sea. The animals may barrow, crawl or remain attached to a substrate.

Benzene (C_6H_6)

It is a colourless liquid hydrocarbon which is prepared from gasoline. Its boiling point is 80.1°C and melting point 5.5°C. It is an aromatic compound which is used as a solvent and for the synthesis of many chemicals.

Beriberi

Beriberi is a nervous system disease caused by the deficiency of vitamin B_1 (thiamin). Symptoms include difficulty in walking, loss of sensation in hands and feet, loss of muscle function, mental confusion, tingling, pain strange eye movement, coma, heart failure, etc. It has been found most common in Far East region where people eat polished rice.

Berkelium (*Symbol* Bk)

It is a soft, silvery white radioactive metallic element with atomic number 97. It is a member of actinides and transuranium element series. It is named after the city of Berkeley (California) where it was discovered in 1949. It has eight known isotopes.

Bernoulli, Daniel (1700-82)

He was a Swiss Mathematician and Physicist of the renowned Bernoulli family. His major contribution was his application of mathematics to mechanics particularly fluid mechanics and also his pioneering work in the field of probability and statistics.

Bernoulli, Daniel

Berry

It is a fleshy fruit with more seeds, for example, grapes and tomatoes. A berry like cucumber which has a hard outer rind is called pepo.

Beryl

It is a hexagonal mineral form of beryllium aluminum silicate, found throughout the world in granites and pegmatites. It may be yellow, green, white, or blue and has been used as gemstone since ages.

Beryl

Beryllium (*Symbol* Be)

It is a grey metallic element of group II of the periodic table, with melting point 1278°C and boiling point 2970°C. It is used in the manufacturing of beryllium-copper alloys, which are used in nuclear reactor.

Bessemer process

It is a process used for making steel from cast iron. In this process, a tilted vessel called Bessemer is used as a converter in which molten iron, carbon and oxygen react to produce steel. The process is named after the British Engineer Sir Henry Bessemer.

Beta iron

It is a non-magnetic allotrope of iron. It exists between 786°C and 900° C.

Beta particle

The term refers to an electron or positron emitted with great velocity during beta decay. A beta particle is more powerful than an alpha particle in terms of penetration but is weaker than gamma radiation.

Betatron

The term is used for an accelerator for producing high energy electrons for purposes such as research, X-rays, etc. The electrons are produced by electromagnetic induction, first developed in 1939 by D.W. Kerst.

Biceps

The term is used for the muscle that runs along the upper arm. It is connected to the radius at one end and the other end is connected to the shoulder bone. It helps in flexing the arm at the elbow joint.

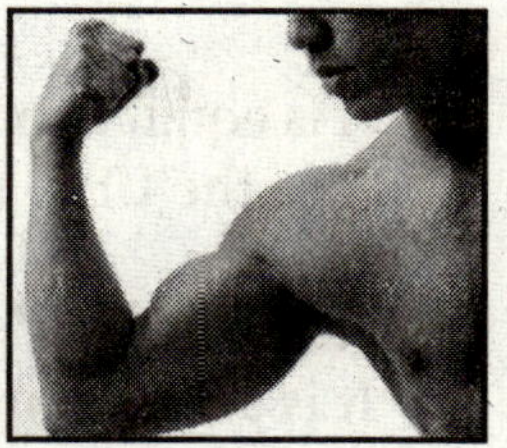

Biceps

Biconcave lens

It is a lens both sides of which is convex while the centre is the thickest. It is so shaped to converge or scatter the light rays. Biconcave lenses have positive focal length and form both real and virtual images.

Biennial

It is used for a plant which has two growing seasons in one life cycle, for example, carrot. In the first year, it builds up food reserves to be used for the production in the next year.

Big bang theory

It is a most widely accepted theory of the origin of the universe that states that all the matter and energy which were concentrated into a dense state of enormous temperature, exploded leading to a creation moment in the past and space and time came into being.

Bilateral symmetry

It refers to a symmetrical arrangement of an organism or body part, along a central axis so that the body is divide into equal halves – right and left. The two halves are the mirror images of each other. It helps in efficient movement.

Bile

It is a greenish-yellow alkaline fluid produced by the liver and stored in the gall bladder. It helps in the digestion and absorption of fats. It also helps in gut muscle contraction.

Billion

It is equal to one million million, 10^{12} the UK and Germany while in the USA and France it is one thousand million, 10^9.

Bimetallic strip

It is a strip consisting of two metals, which have different expansivity, but riveted and welded together to make it bend when heated. When one end is fixed the other end can be made to open and close an electric circuit, for example in a thermostat.

Binary stars

It refers to a pair of stars orbiting around a common centre of mass. Binary star system holds great importance in astrophysics. Alpha centauri and Epsilon are examples of binary stars.

Binary energy

It is the energy required to disassemble the whole into separate parts. It is the energy that binds the proton and neutron of the atomic nucleus. Electron binding energy is the measure of energy required to free electrons from their atomic orbits.

Binoculars

Binoculars are a pair of identical or mirror-symmetrical telescopes mounted side by side and aligned to point accurately in the same direction, designed so help the viewer to use both the eyes at once. Most are designed in a way to be held by both hands.

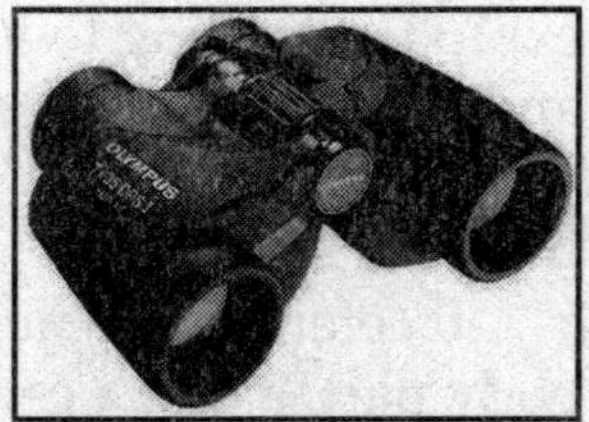

Binoculars

Biochemistry

It is the study of chemical processes in living organisms, especially the structure and function of their chemical components, including the functions and interactions of cellular components such as protein, carbohydrates, lipids and nucleic acids and biomolecules.

Biodegradation

It is defined as the chemical degradation of waste materials by biological influences such as by bacteria. The term is often used in the context of ecology, waste management, biomedicine and natural environment. Now, it is widely used in the context of environmentally friendly products.

Biodiversity

It refers to diversity of life on the earth, including animals, plants and microorganisms in a natural community or habitat. Certain habitats, for example, rainforests are characterised by big diversity, which is facing great threat because of indiscriminate deforestation.

Biogas

It is a gas of a combination of methane and carbon dioxide produced by bacterial fermentation of waste materials such as domestic, industrial and agricultural waste. The decomposition of biogas takes place in specialised equipment. Biogas is now used as a cooking fuel.

Biogas

Biogenesis

The term is used for the principle of the formation of living organisms from parent organisms. Living organisms cannot originate from the non-living materials.

Biogeography

It is the branch of biology that concerns the study of biological distribution of plants and animals.

Bioinformatics

It is a branch of biological science which studies the methods for collection, storage and analysis of biological data related to DNA and protein sequence, including structure, function, pathways and genetic interactions, with the help of computer systems. It also studies algorithms, databases, information systems, structural biology, data mining, software engineering, circuit theory, etc. Bioinformatics attempts to increase the understanding of biological processes.

Biological clock

It denotes an internal mechanism of organisms, presumed to exist in many animals and plants that regulates the periodic changes in various functions and activities in them such as sleep cycle, metabolic changes and photosynthesis in plants.

Biological control

It implies the use of biological means in pests control rather than chemical which is done by breeding disease resistant crop or by using natural enemies of the pest. It is an environmentally sound and effective means of mitigating pests. Sometimes a predator or parasite is used to control the pests. Often insect pests have to be controlled genetically by releasing large number of sterilised male of the species thereby reducing insect population.

Biological control

Biological warfare

The term refers to the use of biological toxins and infectious agents like viruses, bacteria, fungi, and other microorganisms to induce disease and deaths among animals, plants and human beings. Biological warfare is employed to gain strategic advantage over the adversary.

Biology

The branch of science that studies life and living organisms including their origin, evolution, classification, structure, distribution.

Biomass

It represents the total number of living organisms in a given area, for example, the biomass of tigers in Betla National Park.

Biomechanics

It is the science concerned with the study of the structure and function of biological system such as plants, animals and cells by applying the methods and techniques of mechanics. It is also used for the study of properties of certain biological materials such as blood and bone.

Biophysics

It studies the physical aspects of biology, including the various applications of the laws of physics to the study of biology.

Biopsy

It is a medical test in which some tissue of the affected part is removed to determine the cause and extent of a disease. It is a diagnostic test in which a needle is inserted into the organ from where some tissue is extracted for examination.

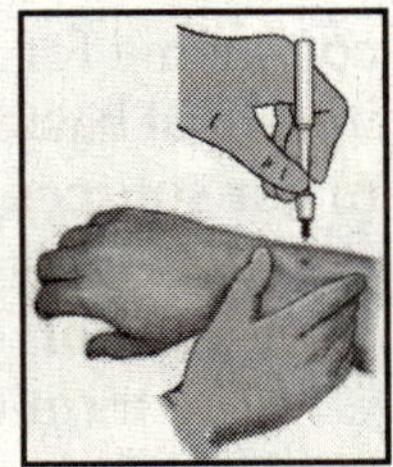

Biopsy

Bioreactor

It is a large stainless steel tank used for growing producer microorganisms for industrial production of enzymes. The tank is sterilized and the levels of temperature, pressure, oxygen and pH are maintained for enzyme production.

Biosensor

It is a device used to detect or measure a chemical compound. It uses immobilized agents such as antibiotics, enzymes, organelles or whole cells. Biosensors are used in diagnostic tests.

Biosphere

The term broadly includes the whole region of the surface area of the earth, the sea and the air with all their inhabiting organisms.

Biotechnology

It concerns the wider applications of biological processes in the field of medicine and industry. Various kinds of antibiotics and vaccines are produced from bacteria and fungi. Genetic engineering can modify bacterial cells to synthesise various hormones, vaccines, etc. Genetic traits of plants and animals can be modified and new traits can be introduced to suit various human needs and requirements with the help of biotechnology.

Biotin

It is a vitamin in the vitamin B complex group and a coenzyme for various enzymes. It is adequately produced by intestinal bacteria, however egg, liver, milk, vegetables are other major sources of biotin.

Birth control

The term means to intentionally control child birth using 'natural' or artificial' methods. Natural methods are used because of moral or religious objections in certain community. Artificial methods include the use of contraceptives and sterilisation of male and female. Birth control is encouraged by government in many countries like India and China where big population is a major problem.

Birth rate

It is the rate at which a particular species produces the offspring. Birth rate is used to measure the reproductive capability of the species. It is defined as the number of birth every year for every 1000 people in the population of a place. It is an important factor to control the population growth.

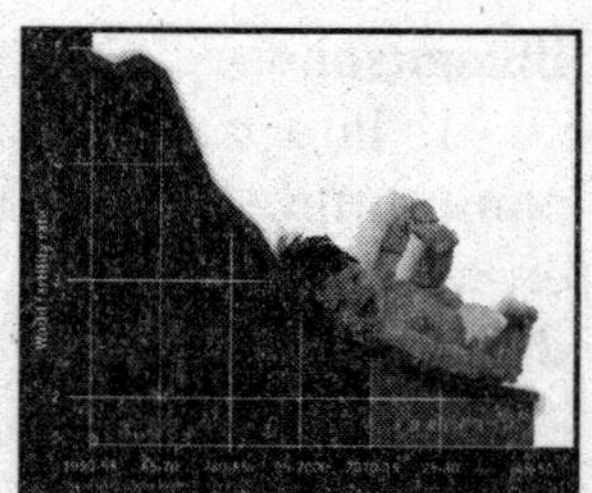

Birth rate

Bismuth (*Symbol* Bi)

It is a pinkish-white crystalline metal in group 15 (formerly VB) of the periodic table. It is extracted by the carbon reduction of its oxide. Its thermal conductivity is lower than any metal except mercury and has high electrical resistance. It is used to make safety devices for fire detection and sprinkler system. Peru, Japan, Mexico, Bolivia and Canada are its major producers in the world.

Bison

It is a large wild animal belonging to the cow family. It has a strong body covered in hair. It is of two types – the North American and the European.

Bison

Bit

It is the basic unit of information used by a computer. Also called binary digit, it is a single digit number in base-2 (either a one or zero).

Bitumen

It is a residual product in petroleum refineries. It is black oily viscous material which is naturally-occurring organic by-product of decomposed organic materials. It is a common binder used in road construction.

Black body

It is a hypothetical body that completely absorbs any radiation of any wavelength falling on it. It reflects no light on normal temperature and thus appears to be black. The intensities of the various wavelengths of radiation emitted by a black body depend only on its temperature.

Black dwarf

It is a theoretical celestial object created when a white dwarf becomes sufficiently cool enough that it no longer can emit light and heat. Black dwarfs are extremely difficult to be detected.

Black hole

It is a region in space with high gravitational field that

no radiation can escape from it. It is believed that black holes are formed when massive stars collapse at the end of their life cycle and can continue to grow by absorbing mass from its surroundings. Black holes are invisible since no light can escape from it.

Blast furnace

It is a furnace where iron ores are smelted and reduced to pig iron. The furnace is a tall refractory-lined cylindrical structure specially made of refractory bricks covered with steel plates. The furnace is charged at the top with the dressed ore, coke and a flux and a blast of hot air is blown from below. The conversion of iron oxide is a reduction process.

Blasting gelatine

It is a high explosive made from nitroglycerine and gun cotton. It is chiefly used for underwater work. It contains about 7 percent of a cellulose nitrate.

Blastula

It is the first stage in the development of an embryo, generally, resembling a hollow ball. In vertebrates, the blastula forms a disc. In mammal, the blastula stage is known as blastocyst.

Bleaching powder

It is a white solid mixture of calcium chlorate, calcium chloride and calcium hydroxide. It is widely used as a bleaching agent for the disinfection of drinking water and swimming water, besides in paper pulps and fabrics.

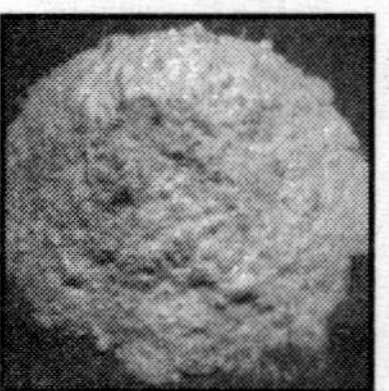

Bleaching powder

Blepharitis

The term is used for the inflammation of the eyelids caused by infection or some allergy.

Blind spot

It is the portion in the retina where blood vessels and nerve fibres enter the retina. This portion has no rods or cones hence it is insensitive to light and visual image can be transmitted from here.

Blood

It is fluid in the body tissue which is contained in a vascular system in vertebrates and serves as a transportation medium in an animal. The heart is responsible for its circulation throughout the body. Blood consists of blood cells and platelets. It is through blood that oxygen and food is supplied to tissues. It also carries hormones throughout the body and acts as a defence system.

Blood

Blood clotting

The term is used for the formation of a mass of semi-solid material at the site of injury which closes the wound and helps in further blood loss. The clotting is formed by the coagulation of blood by a complex process involving clotting factors and platelets.

Blood count

It refers to the number of different cells (red and white blood cells) in per litre of blood.

Blood groups

It represents the classification of human blood based on the presence and absence of certain antigenic proteins in the red blood cells. Human blood is classified in four groups – A, B, AB and O. Blood of one group contains antibodies in the serum that reacts against the antigens of other groups. Incompatibility results in clumping of cells. Blood groups were discovered by Landsteiner in 1900.

Blood pressure

It is pressure exerted through the major arteries of the

body by the flow of blood which is the highest when the ventricles of the heart constrict and thus forcing the blood into the arterial system. The pressure is the lowest when the ventricles relax (diastolic pressure). Normal blood pressure for a young adult human is 120/80 mmHg. It is measured by sphygmomanometer.

Blood sugar

It refers to the amount of glucose present in blood which is generally 80 to 120 mg per 100 ml of blood. This amount may vary. Insulin regulates the amount of glucose in the blood. When the insulin secretion fails, sugar concentration in the blood increases and this condition is called insulin.

Blood transfusion

It means transfusion of blood from a donor to a recipient or a patient who is in need of it because of accident or disease. Blood compatibility and cross matching is very important before the transfusion of blood.

Blood transfusion

Blood vascular system

The term involves tissues and organs involved in the transportation of blood throughout the body. In vertebrates, the vascular system consists of heart and blood vessels.

Blue baby

The term is used to refer an infant who is suffering from a congenital malformation of heart. Blood does not get oxygenated as it does not go into the lungs for purification hence there is no oxygenated blood supply. As a result, the infant turns pale or purple in colour. The patient has to undergo cardiac surgery to correct the condition.

Bluetooth

It is a wireless technology which works within a range of 100 meter. It is designed to replace the cables between cell phones, laptops and other devices such as cordless phones, etc. using 2.4 GHz band.

Blue vitriol

It is a crystalline copper sulphate used as fungicide and also for copper plating. Its chemical formula is $CuSO_4.5H_2O$.

Body cavity

It is the internal cavity presents in all invertebrates and vertebrates which contains all major organs. In vertebrates, this cavity is divided by a transverse septum while in mammals the diaphragm is the septum.

Boiling point

It refers to the temperature at which a liquid transforms to the gaseous phase under a pressure. The boiling point of water under normal pressure is 100°C. The boiling point varies with pressure.

Boiling water reactor

It is a nuclear reactor in which turbine is moved by the force of steam which it is produced by allowing water to boil. Thus, electricity is generated with the help of steam.

Bolometer

It is an instrument used to measure radiant energy. In fact it is a kind of detector used to measure infrared radiation. A bolometer works by heating up as it absorbs the radiation that reaches it.

Boltzmann, Ludwig Eduard (1844-1906)

He was an Austrian Physicist who worked on the kinetic theory of gases and thermodynamics. His greatest achievement was in the development of statistical mechanics. Boltzmann was suffering from depression and he committed suicide in an attack of depression.

Boltzmann, Ludwig Eduard

Bomb calorimeter

It is an instrument used for measuring the calorific value of foods and fuels. The calorific value of constant volume can be calculated from the resulting rise in temperature.

Bond energy

It is the energy associated with a bound in a chemical compound. It is the measure of bound strength in a chemical compound which can be obtained from the heat of atomisation. It is the force which holds together atoms of an element.

Bone

It is the hard connective tissue that forms the skeleton of most vertebrates. They protect and support the various organs in the body, produce blood cells and store minerals. Bones are primarily composed of calcium phosphate. The largest bone in the humans is femur and the smallest bones are auditory ossicles.

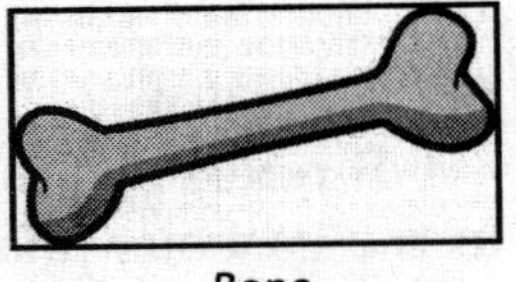

Bone

Bone tissue

It is soft tissue found in the hollow interior of bones which produces red blood cells and is known as red marrow. On an average bone marrow constitutes 4 per cent of the total body mass of humans.

Booster

It implies the following:

1. It is an auxiliary device used to increase force, power, pressure or effectiveness, e.g. a generator or transformer in a circuit to increase or decrease voltage.
2. It is the first stage of multistage space launching vehicle that provides the main thrust for launch or initial flight.
3. In physics, it is a radio-frequency amplifier connected between an aerial and receiver that amplifies weak incoming signals.

Booster dose

It is used for the extra administration of vaccine which is given at a later period to stimulate the effects of previous dose. A booster dose is re-exposer to the immunising antigen cells.

Borax

It is a common household and commercial solid, soluble in water, slightly soluble in ethanol. It is widely used in glass and ceramic industry. It is also used as a mild antiseptic. It is also known as sodium borate or sodium tetra borate.

Boric acid

It is a white a colourless solid soluble in water. It is an acid containing boron and oxygen, used as a weak antiseptic. It is also used in the manufacturing of glass and enamels, lethear, paper, explosives and achesives.

Botany

It relates to the scientific study of plants, including their histology, morphology, ecology, genetics, their geographical distribution, etc.

Botany

Botulism

It is a condition in which central nervous system is badly affected by food poisoning caused by bacteria, sometimes leading to heart and lungs failure. It is caused by consuming badly preserved food.

Boyle's law

The law states that the volume (V) of a given mass of gas at constant temperature is inversely proportional to its pressure (P). It can be expressed as $P \times V$=constant. But when the pressure is doubled, the volume becomes half and vice versa. The law was discovered by Robert Boyle in 1662.

Bragg, Sir William Henry (1862-1942)

He was a British physicist who is credited to have constructed an X-ray spectrometer to measure the wavelength of X-rays. He was awarded the Nobel Prize for Physics in 1915 for his work his work on X-ray crystallography.

Bradycardia

It is a condition in which heartbeat goes down to 50 per minute or less. It may cause unconsciousness.

Braille

It is a system of reading and writing to help the visually impaired people who are unable to read normally. It is named after its inventor Louis Braille.

Brain

It is the one of the major parts of central nervous system encased within the cranium of the skull. It serves as the main coordinating centre for nervous system which receives information from different organs, interprets and again instructs them to work accordingly. It controls movement, thought, memory and feelings. Brain consists of the cerebrum, cerebellum and medulla. Cerebrum is the main part of a human brain which is highly developed.

Brain

Brain death

It is a condition in which brain permanently stops functioning which is manifested in the cessation of breathing and other reflexes controlled by brain, and with zero reading on an electroencephalogram.

Brass

It is an alloy of copper (67%) and zinc (33%). Its colour is yellow. It is widely used in making utensils and household things.

Breathing roots

They are normally upright roots that develop in marshy areas. These are in fact specialised aerial roots that help the plants to breathe air in the habitats which have waterlogged soil. The roots may grow down from the stems or up from typical roots.

Breeding

The term is defined as the process involving sexual reproduction and bearing offspring. Selective breeding is carried out in plants and animals in the field of agriculture to get the desired characteristics of both parents.

Breeding

Breeder reactor

It refers to a nuclear reactor which produces more fissile material than it consumes as it burns by conversion of uranium-238. Earlier it was considered attractive because of its superior fuel economy, later with the discovery of new methods of uranium enrichment that reduced the fuel costs, this method lost importance.

Bronchioles

The term is used for the part of the air passages responsible for controlling air distribution in the vertebrate lungs. They are located at the end of bronchi and ends in alveoli.

Bronze

It refers to a group of alloys of copper and tin, sometimes with lead and zinc present. The amount of tin varies from 1% to 30%. It is widely used in bearings, valves and other machine parts.

Brown dwarf

It is an astronomical object which is faint and is expected to shine about 100 million years before cooling. Its size is intermediate between a large planet and a smaller star. The energy is radiated as electromagnetic radiation.

Brown fat

It is a variety of fat, brown in colour, which is more richly supplied with blood vessels, and has numerous mitochondria. It is found in newborn and hibernating animals. It can more rapidly be converted to heat energy.

Bryophytes

The term includes simple plants which do not have vascular tissue, e.g. mosses, liver worts, etc. Reproduction in them takes place through gametes and spores alternatively.

Bubble chamber

It is a device used for observing the nature and movement of electrically charged particles.

Buccal cavity

The term is used to refer the mouth cavity, the beginning of the alimentary canal bounded by lips, cheeks and gums. It is used both for speaking and digestion.

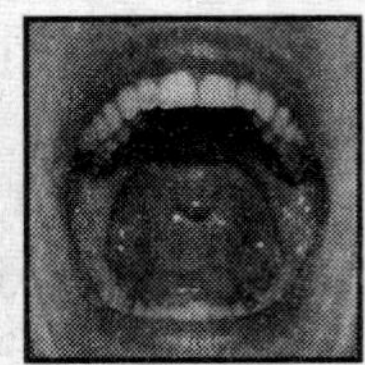

Buccal cavity

Budding

In Biology, it is a method of asexual reproduction in which a new individual is derived from an outgrowth, i.e. bud.

Buffer solution

It is an aqueous solution that has a highly stable pH which does not change significantly even if acid or alkali is added to it. There are two types of buffer – acidic, e.g. carbonic acid and basic like ammonia.

Bulb

It is a short, modified, underground stem surrounded by usually fleshy scale leaves that serves as a store house of food for the shoot for one growing season to the next. It is an underground perennating organ.

Bunsen, Robert Wilhelm (1811-99)

He was a German Chemist and Professor at Kassel who dedicated his early life to researches on arsenic-containing compounds in which he had to lose his one eye in an explosion. Later, he turned to gas analysis and spectroscopy that helped him to discover the elements caesium and rubidium with Kirchhoff. He popularised the use of Bunsen burner.

Bunsen, Robert Wilhelm

Bunsen cell

A cell consisting of zinc cathode immersed in dilute sulphuric acid a carbon anode which is immersed in concentrated nitric acid. It is a primary cell in which the electrolytes are separated by a porous pot. The cell produces an e.m.f. of about 1.9 volts.

Buoyancy

It refers to upthrust on a body immersed in a liquid. It is equal to the weight of the displaced liquid. It was stated by the Greek Mathematician Archimedes.

Burning glass

It is a convex lens that focuses the light rays from the sun and burns the object at the focus.

Burnet, Sir Frank Macfarlane (1899-1985)

He was an Australian virologist who in the early 1930s developed a method of growing influenza virus in chick embryos. He was awarded the Nobel Prize for Medicine in 1960 with Sir Peter Medawar for his contribution in the field of immunological tolerance.

Busen photometer

It is a device used for comparing the light intensities of two sources. It is also called green spot photometer.

Butane

It is gaseous hydrocarbon obtained from petroleum. It is used as fuel for domestic and industrial purposes. It is liquefied under pressure and is used as fuel gas.

Bypass surgery

It is a surgical procedure to remove obstruction in coronary artery by replacing the affected portion with other vessel by grafting a new piece of artery or vein of the patient.

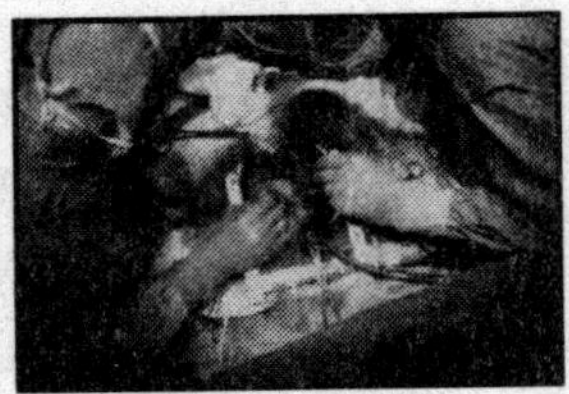

Bypass surgery

By product

It is a compound formed during the production of some other product or substance, usually incidentally. Many commercially useful by products are obtained from various industrial process, for example, propanone is a by-product in the manufacture of phenol.

Byte

The term is used for the subdivision of a word in a computer. Usually, it consists of eight bits. One kilobyte is equal to 1024 bytes.

❑

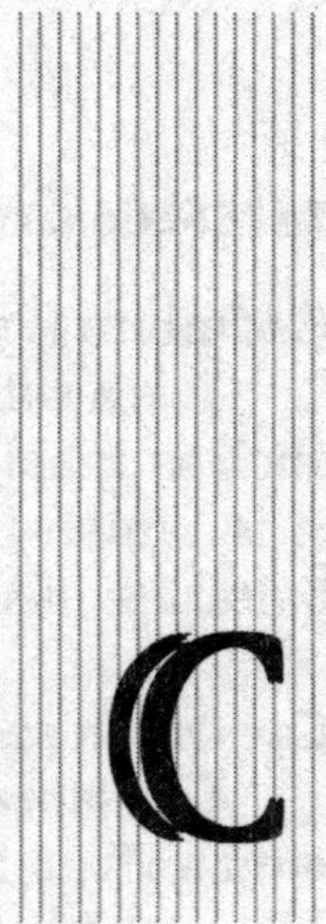

C

It refers to the following:

1. In computer, it is a high level general purpose language. It was developed in 1972, and was superseded in mid 1980s by another computer language C^{++}. It is a fast language which can be used as an assembly to alternative language.
2. In physics, it is a symbol for Coulomb.

Cable television

It is a television broadcasting system in which individual subscribers directly receive the television signals with the help of cables which can be underground or overhead rather than broadcast transmission, unlike the radio broadcasting.

Cactus

It refers to a group of desert plants which are spiny and leafless and has green succulent stem. The plants do not have much commercial value.

Cactus

Cadaver

The term is used for the dead body which is dissected during a post-mortem or kept in a mortuary for medical purpose.

Cadmium (*Symbol* Cd)

It is a soft metal, usually found associated with zinc ores, such as sphalerite, belonging to group 12 of the periodic table. It is bluish in colour. Cadmium is used in bearing alloys, batteries, electroplating and in low melting point alloys.

Caesarean section

Caesarean section is a surgical process in which the woman's abdomen and uterus is cut open to deliver the baby. The procedure is named after Julius Caesar who was born in this way.

Caesium

It is a metallic element belonging to group 1 of the periodic table. It is silver-white in colour the main source of which is carnallite. It is obtained by electrolysis of molten caesium cynide. It is heaviest alkali metal, it has the lowest ionisation potential of all elements.

Caesium clock

It is a type of atomic clock which uses the frequency of radiation absorbed in changing the spin of electrons in two states of the caesium – 133 when it is in a magnetic field. It is a primary frequency standard in which the electronic transitions are used to control the output frequency. The caesium clock is used for the SI unit definition of the second.

Caesium clock

Caffeine

Caffeine is a white crystalline xaynthine alkaloid which acts as a stimulant drug. It is diuretic and is found in varying quantity in coffee, tea and some soft drinks.

Calciferol

The term is used for the group of fat-soluble vitamin D, which helps the body to absorb calcium and phosphorus. Its deficiency causes bone disorders such as rickets, osteomaletia.

Calcification

It refers to the hardening of soft tissues, which is caused by deposition of salts in them. It can be caused by vitamin K deficiency or poor absorption of calcium.

Calcium (Symbol Ca)

It is a soft grey silvery-white element which is the fifth most abundant element by mass found in earth's crust. Its atomic number is 20, melting point 842° C and boiling point 1484°C.

It is an essential element for living organisms required for their proper growth and development. It is particularly important for maintaining healthy and strong bones and normal functions of the body.

Calculus

It is a branch of Mathematics which deals with derivatives, integrals, functions, limits, etc. It is highly useful in solving problems of physics and engineering, besides science and economics.

Calipers

It is a device used to measure the diameter of an object. A calliper can be simple as a compass the tip of which can be adjusted to fit the points to be measured.

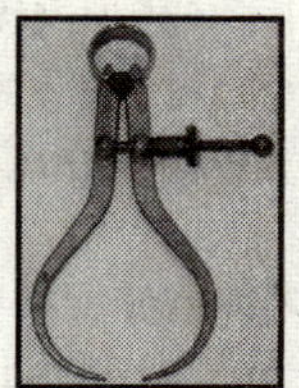

Calipers

Calomel

Also called mercurous chloride, it is a colourless white or brown tasteless odourless compound element. It is used as purgative in medicine, and as insecticide and vermicide.

Calorie

It is defined as the quantity of heat required to raise the temperature of 1 gram of water by 1°C. It is the unit of heat in the CGS system.

Calorific value

It is defined as the heat per unit mass produced by complete combustion of a given substance. It is used to express the energy values of the fuels.

Calorimeter

It is an apparatus used to measure the thermal properties, specific heat capacity, calorific value, latent heat, etc.

Calvin, Malvin (1911-97)

He was a US Biochemist who worked on light-independent reactions of photosynthesis. He was awarded the Nobel Prize for Chemistry in 1961 for his discovery of the Calvin cycle.

Calyx

It refers to the outer whorl of sepals in a flower. It is cup-shaped and encloses the petals, stamens, and carpels. It is green in colour and protects the flower in bud.

Calyx

Camberian

It is the earliest geological period of the Palaeozoic era which is estimated to have begun about 542 million years ago. Marine animals appeared this period.

Camel

It is ruminating four-footed animal which is adapted for life in deserts. It has a big hump on its back which stores fat. A camel can survive for months without water. It is said the 'ship of desert'.

Camera

It is an optical device used to get still pictures. It consists of a light-proof box which has lens at one end and a plate or film at the other end, which when exposed to an image the image is formed on the light sensitive film.

Camphor

It is a white crystalline compound having a characteristic odour associated with its use in mothballs. It is volatile and is obtained from Formosan camphor tree. However, it can also be synthesised.

Cancer

It refers to a disorder of cell growth resulting from a loss of cell cycle control which destroys the surrounding healthy tissues. They multiply more rapidly than the healthy cells and spread to other parts either through blood or lymph. Causes include smoking, radiation, viruses and other chemical agents.

Candela

It is the SI unit of the luminous intensity.

Capacitance

It is the property of a conductor that refers to its ability to store electric charge. It is measured in farads.

Capacitor

It is a device used for temporarily storing electrical charge. It is used in electrical circuits, for example, television sets, computer, radio sets, automobiles, ignition systems, etc.

Capacitor

Capillary

It refers to the following:

1. It is the thinnest blood vessel in the vertebrates' circulatory system.
2. It refers to a tube with small diameter.

Capitulum

In botany, it refers to a type of flowering shoot commonly found in the plants of the Compositae family, where the tip of the shoot is surrounded by a ring of bracts and appears as a single flower, e.g. sunflower, daisy, etc.

Capsule

It denotes the following:

1. In animal anatomy, it is membrane that encloses certain organs, e.g. kidneys, spleen, etc.
2. In botany, it refers to a dry fruit which scatters its seeds when ripe.
3. In microbiology, it is a thick gelatinous layer that surrounds the cell walls of certain bacteria, acting like a protective cover.

Carat

It is used for the following:

1. It is a unit of mass equal to 0.200 gm, largely used to measure the masses of precious stones, like diamond, and other gemstones.
2. It is used to express the purity of gold. Pure gold is 24-carat gold. 18 carat gold means out of 24 parts 18 parts is gold and remaining usually used is copper.

Carbide

It represents a compound of carbon with other electropositive metals such as silicon carbide, calcium carbide, aluminium carbide, etc. These substances are generally hard materials and some of them are used as abrasives.

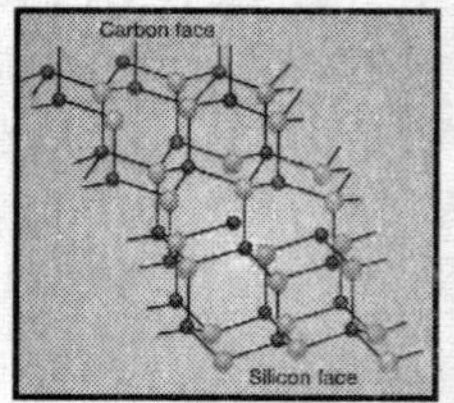

Carbohydrates

It is one of the major organic compounds and an important source of energy for plants and animals. It is very important for the growth and metabolism of living beings. Its main sources are sugars, including glucose and sucrose, and starch.

Carbon (Symbol C)

The basic element in all organic compounds, it is a non-metallic element, which has atomic number 6; atomic weight 12.01; melting point – 3350°C and boiling point – 4827°C. It has two allotropic forms – diamond and graphite. It is fundamental to all living organisms.

Carbon assimilation

It refers to the process of photosynthesis in plants in which plants incorporate carbon from atmospheric carbon dioxide into organic molecules.

Carbonation

It refers to the solution of carbon dioxide in a liquid, e.g. water, under pressure.

Carbon black

It is fine carbon powder produced when hydrocarbons are burned in the absence of sufficient air. It is widely used in rubber and plastic industry.

Carbon black

Carbon cycle

The term refers to the whole system of carbon circulation and recycling in nature. It is one of the major cycles of chemical elements in the environment. In the process of respiration, plants and animals produce carbon dioxide which is absorbed by plants and they convert it into carbohydrates in the process of photosynthesis and release oxygen in the atmosphere. The released oxygen is used by plants and animals during respiration and again carbon is released in the atmosphere. Carbon dioxide is also produced by the decaying of plants and animals and that too returns to atmosphere.

Carbon dating

It is a scientific method to estimate the age of material of archaeological importance having biological origin, e.g. plants and fossils. The atmosphere contains certain amount of radioactive C^{14} formed as a result of cosmic radiation which is absorbed by the living organisms. C^{14} has a half-life (decays to half the strength) of 5,730 years. The strength of C^{14} in plants and fossils are compared with the expected strength of C^{14} in the atmosphere. The ratio of C^{14}/C^{12} indicates the time elapsed since the death of the material. Also known as radio carbon dating, this technique was developed by Willard F. Libby in 1949 who was later awarded the Nobel Prize for Chemistry in 1960.

Carbon footprint

The term has been defined as the total set of greenhouse gas emission caused by an organisation, event, product and person as a result of their various activities. It is measured as the mass of carbon dioxide equivalent, emitted per year and their impacts on greenhouse effect and finally on global warming. Reduce, reuse and recycle, apart from promoting the use of public transportation, forestation, etc. are a few methods suggested to reduce carbon footprint.

Carbon monoxide

It is a colourless, odourless gas, formed by the incomplete combustion of carbon. It is highly toxic and flammable, melting point is 199°C; boiling point is 191.5°C. It is a good reducing agent and is used in several metallurgical processes.

Carborundum

It is a black hard solid compound prepared by heating silicon oxide and carbon in an electric furnace. It is used as an abrasive.

Carburettor

It is a device used to blend air and fuel for an internal combustion engine, prior to explosion. In carburettor, the fuel is completely broken into the minute particles, vaporised, and mixed with the air in proper ratio.

Carburettor

Carcinogen

It is a substance that produces cancer in human beings, for example, tobacco, chemicals and radiation.

Carcinoma

It is a medical term used for any malignant cancer that arises from epithelial cell. Carcinoma affects surrounding tissues and organs and may spread to lymph nodes and other sites.

Cardiac arrest

It can be defined as an abrupt cessation of normal circulation of blood due to failure the heart of in pumping blood around the body thereby stopping the supply of oxygen to different parts.

Cardiac muscle

It is a special type of muscle capable of voluntary rhythmic movement. It is peculiar to the vertebrate heart.

Cardiac pacemaker

It is a small battery-operated device implanted under the skin near the heart to help control the heartbeats.

Cardiogram

It is a graphic record or trace that shows the pattern of heartbeat, produced by electrocardiograph. It is used to treat the heart disorder.

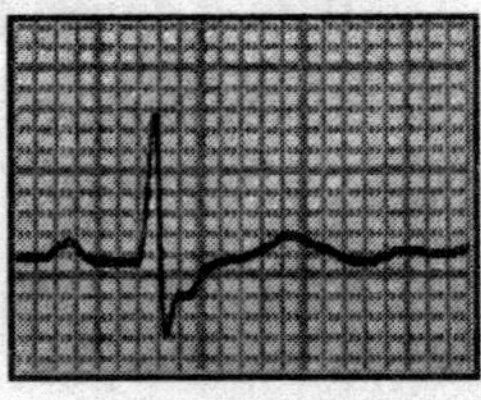

Cardiogram

Carology

It is a medical speciality dealing with the disorders of the heart, including its structure and functions.

Carnivore

It is used to refer the animals that eat flesh as they have the strong powerful jaws and well-developed canine teeth for tearing and eating the flesh, for example, lions, wolves, etc.

Carrier

It denotes the following:

1. In medicine, a person or an animal which transmits a disease without getting affected.
2. In genetics, the term is used for the parents who carry the recessive genes without showing any symptoms of the disease.
3. In physics, an electromagnetic wave of specified frequency and amplitude, emitted by a radio transmitter, to carry information

Cartilage

It is a flexible connective tissue that forms the skeleton in vertebrates, e.g. embryo which is replaced by bone in mature animals. The cartilage gives shape to some organs like ear.

Cartography

It is the art of drawing maps and charts based on the information gathered from survey, aerial photographs or from any other sources.

Cassowary

It is a large flightless bird with horny headcrest, largely found in New Guinea and Queensland. They are swift runners and they can swim as well. They have rudimentary wings.

Cassowary

Case hardening

The term is used to refer the hardening of the surface layer of steel, mainly for tools and other mechanical components. The most widely used method is to carburize the surface layer by heating the metal or by diffusion of nitrogen into the surface layer.

Casein

It is a phosphate-containing proteins found in milk. It is an easily digested food for the young mammals.

Cast iron

Also called pig iron, it is an impure iron produced from the roasting of iron ores in blast furnace. It is poured in sand moulds to make castings. It contains 1.8% to 4.5% carbon.

Catalysis

It describes the process of changing the rate of a chemical reaction caused by catalyst.

Catalyst

It is the agent that increases the rate of a chemical reaction without itself undergoing any permanent change. A catalyst may be positive or negative, the positive accelerates while the latter retards the process. The negative catalysts are used to slow down the reaction process.

Cataract

It is a medical condition that affects the lens of the eyes leading to the gradual loss of sight. It is corrected by surgery or implanting of lens. It is caused mainly by diabetes and ageing.

Catheter

It is a tube which is inserted into the body cavity for injection or the withdrawal of fluids.

Cathetometer

The term is fitted with a telescope or microscope which is fitted with a cross wires in the eyepiece and mounted in a way that it can slide along graduated scale. Cathetometers are used to give accurate measurements of length.

Cathode rays

The term is used for streams of electrons emitted from the cathode of a discharge tube or a vacuum tube. This is the result of an electric discharge that takes place in the vacuum tube.

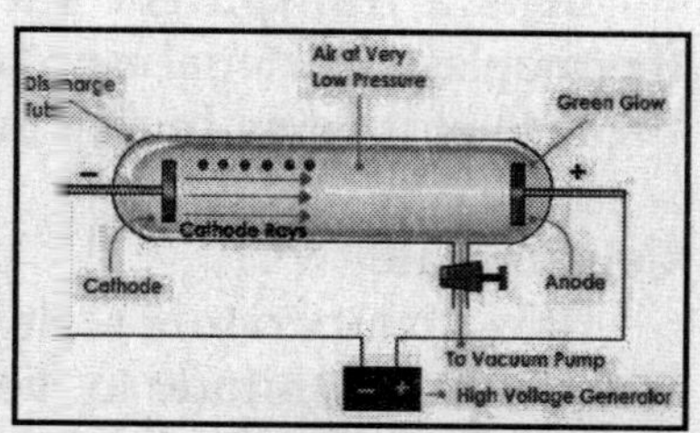

Cathode rays

CD ROM (Computer Disc Read Only Memory)

It is a device used in computer to provide access to a large amount of read-only data. It is a plastic disc with a spiral track, about three miles long which may contain about 6.50 megabytes of data in any form such as text, sound, images or a mixture of various forms of data. CD ROM is widely used for the storage and archiving of data.

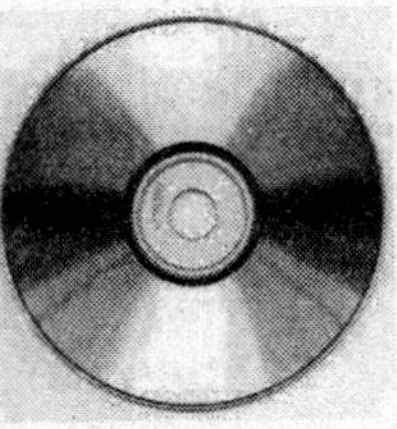

CD ROM

Celestial mechanics

It is a branch of Astronomy which studies the motions and forces between the celestial bodies based on the Newton's Law of Motion and Law of Gravitation besides the General Theory of Relativity.

Cell

It is used to refer the following:

1. In biology, a unit of life consisting of cytoplasm, mitochondria, ribosomes, etc. However, there are differences between plant cells and animal cells.
2. In chemistry, a system in which two electrodes are in contact with an electrolyte.

Cell division

It is defined as the formation of two or more daughter cells from a single mother cell, passing through various stages like division of nucleus, cytoplasm and cell separation.

Celluloid

It is a transparent substance, widely used earlier as thermoplastic material especially for film, but now discontinued because of it being highly inflammable.

Celsius scale

It is a temperature scale in which the degree Celsius (0°C) is equal in magnitude to the Kelvin. The melting point of ice (0°C) is the lower fixed point and boiling point of water (100° C) is the upper point and the scale between these two temperatures is divided in 100 degrees. It is named after the Swedish Astronomer Andres Celsius who devised it in 1942.

Cement

It is a substance used as a bonding material in building construction. It consists of calcium silicates and aluminium silicates, when this mixture is mixed with water and sand, it sets after a few hours and becomes hard.

Central nervous system

It is one of the major systems in the vertebrates that consists of brain and spinal cord and is responsible for the coordination and control of all neural functions in them.

Centrifugal force

It is defined as the outward force which acts on a rotating body towards the centre. It is just the opposite of the centripetal force which is the radial force that keep the body moving in its circular path. These two forces are equal and opposite.

Centrifuge

It is a device used for separating solid or liquid particles of different densities by rotating them in a horizontal circle. It works on centrifugal force.

Ceramics

Ceramics are metal silicates, oxides, nitrites, etc. produced by treating non-metallic inorganic materials such as clay at high temperature.

Cerebellum

It is the part of the vertebrate brain that controls and coordinates the muscular activities and maintains the balance of body.

Cerebellum

Cerebrum

It is the largest part of the vertebrate brain which consists of the two cerebral hemispheres. It controls all voluntary activities and integrates complex sensory and neural functions. It is the centre of intelligence.

Cerussite

It is an ore of lead, usually of secondary origin, formed by the weathering of galena. Pure cerussite is white but it may be grey due to the presence of impurities. It occurs in the USA, Spain and Africa.

Cervix

It is the narrow part of an organ. The neck of the uterus in women is also called cervix.

Catacea

It refers to the order of aquatic mammals which includes whales, dolphins and porpoise.

Catacea

CGS system

It is a system of units based on gram, centimetre and second. Derived from the metric system, it has now been replaced by the SI units.

Chadwick, Sir James (1891-1974)

He was the British Physicist who discovered neutron in 1932. In 1935, he was awarded the Nobel Prize for his work in the field of Science.

Chain reaction

It is a fission reaction, which is a continuous reaction and can be controlled by moderators. This reaction is initiated by the splitting of some atomic nuclei, which in turn split other, releasing free neurons. It is self-sustaining.

Charcoal

It is a porous form of carbon produced by heating or burning some organic material such as wood or sugar in the absence of air. Since it is porous, it is used in gas mask to absorb poisonous gases. There are several types of charcoal depending on the source, e.g. animal charcoal coconut charcoal, etc.

Charge

It refers to the property of certain atoms or molecules that gives rise to an interaction between them which is called electrical. Charge occurs in two forms popularly known as positive and negative charge that shows the kind of interaction between the particles. The unit to measure charge is coulombs. Proton has a positive charge while electron is negatively charged.

Charles' Law

It states that all gases expand at constant pressure by 1/273 of their volume at 0°C for each 1°C rise in temperature or at constant pressure the volume of a fixed mass of gas is proportional to the absolute temperature. It can be expressed as $V1/T1=V_2/T_2$ where V = Volume and T= Temperature.

Chemical change

It is defined as the permanent change in a substance as a result of rearrangement of atoms in its molecules. Sometimes the change is not reversible.

Chemical control

It refers to the use of chemicals to kill pests that destroy agricultural products or are harmful to human beings in anyway.

Chemical control

Chemical engineering

It concerns with the study of the design, manufacture and operation of plant and machinery in industrial chemical processes.

Chemical equation

It refers to an equation which shows a chemical reaction of elements or compounds with the help of symbols:

$3H_2 + N_2 = 2NH_3$

Chemical reaction

It refers to a change which results in the formation of one or more chemical elements or compounds breaking old bonds and forming new bonds. In most of the cases reactions are regarded as irreversible since back reaction is almost negligible.

Chemical warfare

It implies the use of toxic chemicals in warfare or military operation against the enemy. Different kinds of chemicals have been designed for the warfare such as pulmonary agents, nerve agents, blister agents, etc. Chemical warfare agents cause mass destruction.

Chemistry

It refers to the study of the elements and the compounds they form including the various branches like biochemistry, inorganic chemistry, geochemistry, organic chemistry, etc.

Chemotherapy

It refers to the use of chemicals especially drugs in the treatment of diseases, for example, cancer. It directly destroys the organisms and check new growth in the body.

Chicken pox

It is a contagious disease mostly affecting the children. It is caused by a virus. It is characterised by high fever and skin rashes.

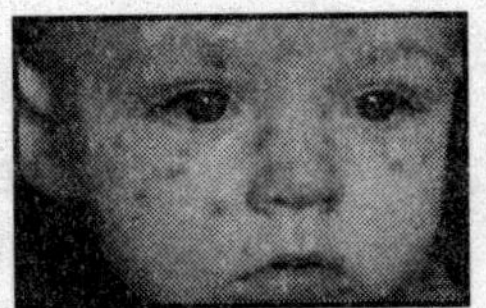

Chicken pox

China clay

It is a soft white clay chiefly composed of the mineral kaolinite. It is used in the manufacture of ceramics, paper, rubber, etc. and also as a constituent of medicines.

Chlorophyll

It refers to the pigment responsible for the green colour of plants. It has a significant role in the process of photosynthesis in which plants make their food in the presence of sunlight.

Chloroplast

It refers to chlorophyll-containing organelles found in plant cells which are undergoing photosynthesis. Chloroplasts are lens-shaped.

Choke

It refers to a coil of wire used in radio and television circuits to impede the passage of audio and radio frequency currents. Its inductance is high and resistance is low.

Cholera

It is an epidemic disease caused by bacteria and is spread by food or water. Symptoms include vomiting, loose motion leading to severe dehydration which if not treated well can be fatal.

Cholesterol

It is a sterol or fat found in animal tissues and also in some plants and algae. It is produced in the liver and is a main constituent of blood plasma. Its role is important for the production of hormones. Its high concentration in blood causes coronary thrombosis in man which damages the blood vessels.

Chordate

It belongs to a phylum of animals containing vertebral column.

Chromatography

It is a technique used for analysing and separating mixtures of gases and liquids. It is also used for separating dissolved substances.

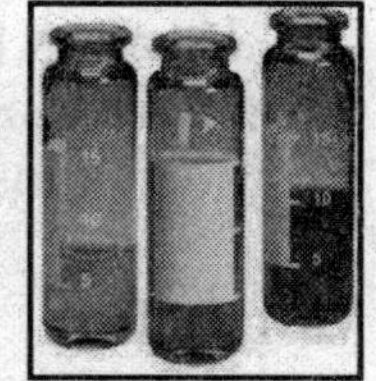
Chromatography

Chromium (*Symbol* Cr)

It is a hard silvery metallic element in transitional block of the periodic table having atomic number 24, atomic weight 52, melting point 1857°C and boiling point 2672°C. Its main ore is chromite. It is used in making alloys steel besides as a shiny decorative electroplated coating in some chromium compounds. At normal temperature chromium is corrosion-resistant.

Chromosome

It is a thread-like genetic structure found i of plant and animal cells. It consists of nucleopr acid and DNA and they carry the genes in lin Chromosomes occur in pairs, each consisting of tw There are 23 pairs in human beings, 22 matched pair of sex chromosomes. Down's syndrome structural abnormalities in the chromosomes.

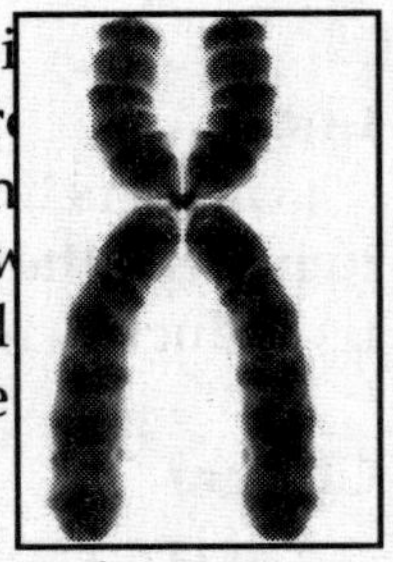
Chromosome

Chromospheres

It is the layer of the sun's atmosphere just above the photosphere visible only during the total lunar eclipse. It is about 10,000 km thick and has an even temperature of 20,000 K.

Chronometer

It is an accurate clock used in navigation. It helps in finding out longitude.

Cilium

It is a minute hair-like structure up to 10 μ long, found on the surface of cells. Cilia usually occur in groups and help in locomotion.

Circulatory system

It refers to the group of organs which together serve to transport materials throughout the body. It includes heart, arteries, veins and lymph.

Cirrhosis

It is a chronic disease of the liver caused by the infection and alcoholism. It destructs liver cells and replaces them with fibrous tissues.

Citric acid

It is an organic acid found in citrus group of fruits, e.g. lime. It has an important role in the metabolism.

Climatology

It refers to the study of climate, its causes and changes, broadly including the causes of climatic difference and various application used to solve it, besides solar radiation, ocean currents, wind and water mass, which have great influence on human life.

Clinical thermometer

It is a clinical thermometer used to measure body temperature. It is used by doctors and nurses.

Clone

The term is used for a group of cells or organisms produced from a single cell. All members of a particular have identical genetic make-up.

Coal

It is a fossil fuel found in sedimentary rocks. It consists mainly of carbon or hydrocarbons which are turned as coal as a result of high temperatures and pressures. It is a complex process which takes millions of years. Coals are of different kinds, namely peat, lignite, bituminous coal and anthracite.

Coal

Coal gas

It is a fuel gas formed by the destructive distillation of coal, the by-products of the process being coke and coal tar. It contained hydrogen (50%), methane (35%) and carbon monoxide (8%). In 19th and 20th century, it was a major source of energy but its use declined with the increasing availability of natural gas.

Cobalt (*Symbol* Co)

It is a light grey element in group VIII of the periodic table, with atomic number 27; atomic weight 58.9; melting point

1495°C; boiling point 2870°C. Cobalt is ferromagnetic and is extracted from cobaltite, smaltite and erythrite. Usually, cobalt is alloyed for use. Cobalt salts are used in glass, tiles and pottery. Artificially produced cobalt-60 is used in the treatment of cancer.

COBOL

It is a common business-oriented computer language, developed in the early 1960s. It is a data processing language widely used in the field of commerce.

Cocaine

It is drug found in the leaves of coca plant which stimulates the central nervous system. Originally, it was used as a local anaesthetic. Its effects are similar to the amphetamines.

Cocaine

Cocoon

It is a protective coverings for the larvae or eggs produced insects, for example, the earthworms secrete cocoon for the eggs and silkworm moths spin cocoon for the pupae.

Coercive force

It refers to the magnetizing force required to reduce the flux density in a magnetic material to zero.

Cohesion

It denotes the following:

1. In Physics, it is the force of attraction that is between the molecules and that hold them together.
2. In Botany, it is the union of identical parts, e.g. the fusion of petals in some flowers.

Coke

It is a form of carbon produced by the destructive distillation of coal, mainly used in blast furnaces and other metallurgical and chemical processes which require carbon. It is also used as domestic fuel.

Collimator

It inplies the following:

Collimator

1. It is a small fixed telescope attached to a large astronomical telescope that assists in lining up the large one onto the desired celestial body.
2. It is a device used for producing a parallel beam of particle or wave radiation. Collimators utilize a system of silts or apertures.

Colorimeter

It is an instrument used for comparing or reproducing colours. Colorimeters are monochromatic or trichromatic.

Colostrum

It refers to a liquid produced in the mammals before and just after the child birth. The liquid is rich in nitrogen, antibodies and vitamins.

Colour blindness

The term is used for the vision disorder in which colours are confused. The most common type is the one in which one finds it difficult to distinguish between red and green colours. It is a hereditary disease transmitted by the sex chromosomes from the mother to son.

Coma

It refers to the following:

1. It is a condition charactersed by deep consciousness without any response to stimuli. It can be caused by a disease, injury or alcoholism.
2. It refers to a nebulous cloud of gas and dust that surrounds the nucleus of comet.

Comet

It represents a member of the solar system that moves around the sun in an orbit. A comet has a nucleus of ice and dust, surrounded by the coma of dust and frozen gases and a tail. Halley's Comet is very famous because of its regular appearance in every 76 years.

Communication satellite

It refers to an unmanned artificial satellite orbiting the earth relaying television and radio signals between far-off ground stations on the earth. The satellites are placed into a geostationary orbit by rocket.

Communication satellite

Compact dick

It is a metal dick which has a digital recording of audio information. It provides a high quality recording and reproduction of music, speeches, etc.

Compost

It is a mixture of decaying organic substance from plants which is used as manure.

Compound eye

The term is used for the eye of insects and crustaceans, consisting of numerous visual units called ommatidia.

Compound lens

It is a lens which is a combination of two or more lenses.

Condensation

It can be defined as a process which turns vapour or gas into a liquid.

Condenser

The term is used for the following:

1. A device that is used to turn vapour or gas into a liquid.
2. In optics, it refers to a mirror or lens which concentrates

the light diverging from a compact source. It is mostly used in a microscope or film projector.

Conductor

It is a substance which has high thermal and electrical conductivity. Metals are good conductor of heat.

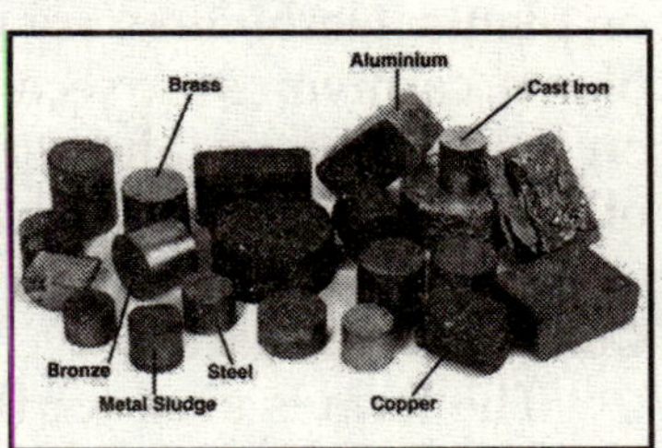

Conductor

Configuration

It implies the arrangement of atoms in a molecule. Also the arrangements of electrons in atomic orbital in an atom is called configuration.

Congenital

It refers to a condition, disease or disorder present since birth. It may be due to injury, infection, or chemical or genetic factors, e.g. Down's syndrome, thalidomide, etc.

Conjunctiva

It is a delicate membrane that covers the front part of the eye. The reflex blink mechanism keeps it clean. A disease called conjunctivitis is caused by the infection of the conjunctiva.

Conservation

The term can be defined as the rational use of earth's natural resources so as to sustain it for the generation to come. It can be done by searching the alternative of food and fuel supplies, creating an awareness towards the dangers of pollution and preservation of natural habitats.

Constellation

The term is used for a group of stars forming a particular pattern or shape in the sky. There are 88 constellations most of them named after animals and mythological characters, Crux being the smallest and Hydra is the largest constellation.

Consumer

It refers to an organism that feeds directly or indirectly on plants. Herbivores are primary consumers who feed upon plants, carnivores are secondary consumers since they survive on the herbivores and tertiary consumers which feed upon other carnivores.

Contagious disease

The term is used for the disease which spreads by direct contact.

Continuum

It refers to a system of continuous series of components forming a frame of reference. According to Einstein the three dimensions of space and the fourth dimension of time make a four-dimensional continuum.

Contractile root

The term is used for modified adventitious roots that develop from the base of the stem of a bulb or corn.

Control mechanism

It is a mechanism that helps to maintain the internal environment either by regulating a biological process or enzyme-controlled reaction.

Convection

It is defined as a process by which heat is transferred from one part of another by the motion of the heated molecules itself. Molecules when come in contact with the heat become more hot and less dense as they expand, and then they rise. They are replaced with the colder molecules.

Converging lens

It is a lens that focuses a beam of light that passes through it. Such a lens is called concave lens which is thicker at its centre than its edge.

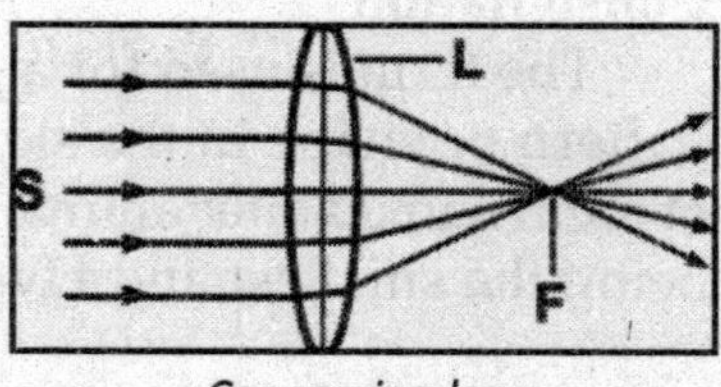

Converging lens

Converter

It refers to the following:

1. A computer device that converts the information coded in one form into some other form.
2. An electrical device that converts alternating current into direct current or vice versa.

Convertor reactor

It is a nuclear reactor that converts fertile material like thorium – 232 into fissile material, e.g. uranium-233. A convertor reactor can be used for power generation.

Convex

It is used for an object which is curved outwardly, e.g. convex lenses. A convex lens is thicker at the centre than the exterior surface. It is a converging lens.

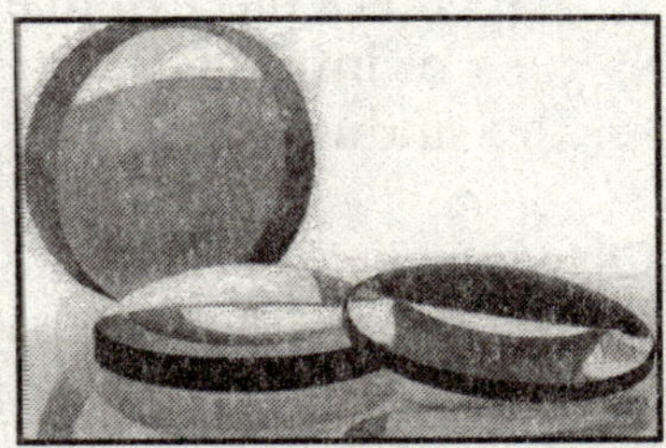

Convex

Coolant

It is a fluid used in cooling to extract heat from one source and then transfer it to another, either to control the temperature or to extract energy. Coolants are used in nuclear reactor and car engine.

Copper (*Symbol* Cu)

It is a red-brown transition element, atomic Number 29; atomic weight 63.55; melting point 1084°C; and boiling point 2563°C. Copper is an excellent conductor of electricity and heat. It is malleable and ductile. Main ores of copper include cuprite, chalcopyrite, malachite and azurite. Copper is extensively used to make electric cables and wires, and also used in alloys such as bronze and brass.

Coral

The term represents the deposits of calcium carbonate formed from the remains of marine invertebrates. Coral forms the coral reef which is common in tropical seas.

Cordite

It is an explosive mixture produced from cellulose nitrate and nitroglycerin.

Core

The term is used for the following:

1. It refers to the part of nuclear reactor where the nuclear reaction takes place.
2. It is the central region of a star.
3. It is used for the devices used in certain computers to make the memory.
4. It is a piece of magnetic material around which a coil of insulated wire is wound that helps to increase its inductance.

Cornea

It refers to the transparent layer of tissue which makes the front part of vertebrate eye. It refracts the light entering into the eye.

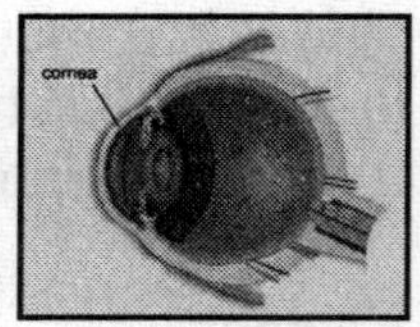

Cornea

Corona

It is the outer part of the sun's atmosphere which is cooler and extends several million kilometres into space. Also the irregular halo surrounding the sun, seen only during the solar eclipse, is called corona.

Coronary vessels

The term is used for the blood vessels - coronary arteries and coronary veins - that supply blood to the heart of the muscles itself.

Corrosion

It refers to the chemical or electrochemical attack on the surface of a metal that causes gradual destruction of metal surface.

Cortex

In Zoology, it is the outer layer of some organs such as adrenal glands, kidneys and cerebral hemispheres.

Corundum

It is natural aluminium oxide which is as hard as diamond. It is colourless and transparent when it is pure but presence of other elements gives it some colour. It occurs in both metamorphic and igneous rock. It is the second hardest mineral after diamond. It is used as abrasive.

Cosmic rays

The term is used for the rays, consisting of mostly protons, falling on the earth's surface from outer space. The origin of the cosmic rays is not known.

Cosmology

It concerns with the science of the origin, nature and evolution of the universe. There are many theories concerning the topic exist, namely big bang theory, steady state theory, etc.

Coulomb (*Symbol* C)

It is the SI unit of electric charge that is equal to the charge transported by a current of one ampere in one second.

Counter

It refers to a device used for detecting and counting ionising particles or radiation, for example, Geiger-Muller counter.

CPU

It is the main operating part of a computer which includes the Control Unit (CU) and the arithmetic/logic unit. It has a significant role in the execution of a program.

Cranium

It is the outer protective part of the vertebrate skull which encloses the brain.

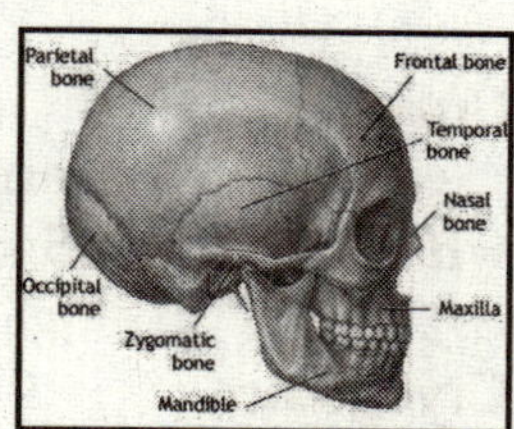

Cranium

Cretaceous

It is geological period of the Mesozoic era which extends from about 144 million years to about 65 million years ago when dinosaurs existed on the Earth. Angiosperm plants first appeared on the earth in this period.

Critical angle

It refers to the angle at which the total internal reflection occurs. It is the least angle of incidence.

Crop rotation

It can be defined as an agriculture practice in which different crops are cultivated on an area of land in a particular period of time in succession to maintain the fertility of the soil. Legumes are good for this purpose as they are a good source of nitrogen for the soil.

Cross pollination

In botany, it refers to the transfer of pollen from the anther of one flower to the stigma of another flower of a different plant.

Crown glass

In Chemistry, it is used to refer a variety of hard glass which is highly transparent for light. It is used in optical instruments.

Crude oil

It is a naturally occurring thick black liquid consisting of mixture of gases, liquid and solid hydrocarbons, formed in the rock. It is found in unrefined form and is refined by fractional distillation to get petrol, etc.

Crust

It is the outermost layer of the earth which is about 45 km thick.

Crust

Cryogenics

It refers to the scientific study of the production of very low temperatures and their effects.

Cryolite

It is a mineral form of sodium aluminoflouride. It is a rare form of the mineral found mainly in Greenland.

Cryometer

It is a thermometer used to measure the low temperatures.

Crystal

It is a solid which has a regular polyhedral shape with orderly three-dimensional arrangements of its atoms or molecules with smooth faces.

Crystallography

It refers to the scientific study of crystal, its forms and structure.

Culture

It is used for cells of microorganisms - either of plant or animal origin - grown under specific condition - for scientific study or purpose.

Curie (*Symbol* Cm)

It is a unit of radioactivity, equal to 3.7×10^{10} disintegration per second. It is named after Pierre Curie

Cushining's syndrome

It is a condition caused by the excess secretion of corticosteroid hormones in the body. Its symptoms include weight gain, excess growth of body and facial hair, high blood pressure, loss of minerals from the bones and mental problems.

Cuticle

It is used for the following:

1. In Zoology, it refers to a layer of horny non-cellular material covering, usually, made of protein. In some arthropods, it serves as skeleton.
2. In Botany, it is the continuous waxy layer covering the aerial parts of a plant. It helps to prevent water loss in plants.

Cyclone

It refers to an area of low pressure, commonly referred to as depressions which cause devastating storm.

Cyclotron

It is a device in which positively charged particles fed into the centre are accelerated in an outward spiral path. A magnetic field applied at right angles makes them follow curved paths.

Cytology

It concerns with the study of the structure and functions of cells. It helps in the diagnosis of various diseases, e.g. cancer.

Cytoplasm

It is a complex fluid which is the basis of life in both plants and animals. It is found in cells which make up the protoplasm of the cell, plasma membrane and nucleus.

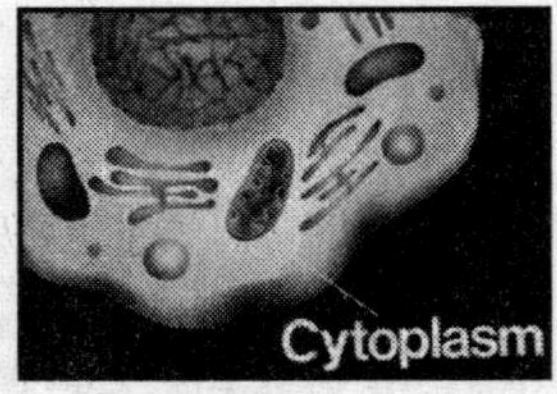

Cytoplasm

❑

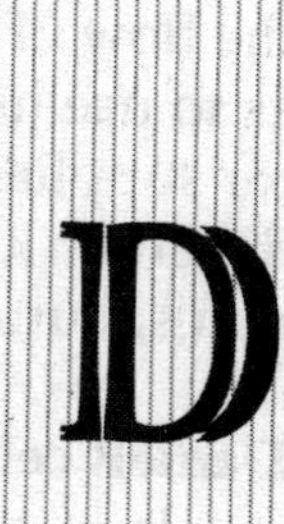

D

In Chemistry, it is the symbol for deuterium.

In Mathematics, it is used as a symbol for deci-.

Dactylography

It is the scientific study of finger prints widely used in the fields of criminology and forensic science to identify people particularly criminals.

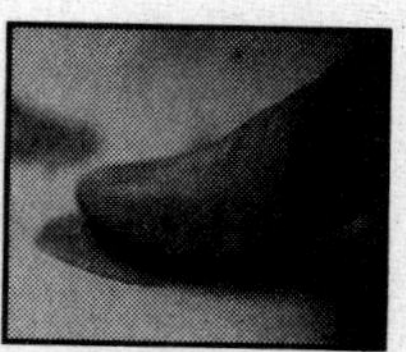

Dactylography

Dalton

In Physics, it is used as an alternative name for atomic mass unit.

Dalton, John (1766-1844)

British Chemist and Physicist who is widely known for his studies on colour blindness as a condition. In 1801, he formulated his law of partial pressure but is best remembered for his famous Dalton's Atomic Theory.

Dalton's atomic theory

It is is a theory of chemical combination, stated by John Dalton, which postulates that matter is composed of particles commonly known as atoms, which is indivisible. Atoms cannot be created nor can they be destroyed.

Dam

It a huge structural barrier built across a river to contain the flow of its water, or to divert its flow with purposes such as to use its water for irrigation or navigation, to store water for supplies to people and to produce electricity. Dams are of different kinds, namely gravity dams, masonry dams, arch dams, buttress dams, etc.

Daniell cell

It is a primary voltaic cell which has a copper positive electrode and a negative electrode of zinc amalgam. It has emf 1.08 volts. It is named after its inventor British Chemist John Daniell.

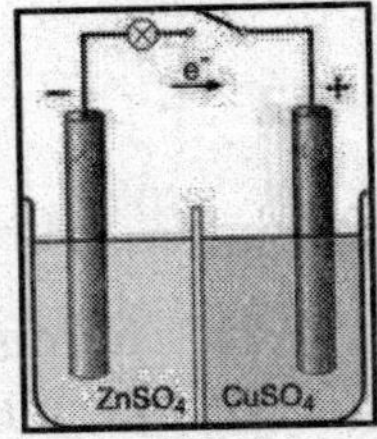

Daniell cell

Dark matter

The term is used for the matter which cannot be detected by current instruments though its existence is inferred by its gravitational forces. Dark matter constitutes 90-99% of the universe.

Dark reaction

It refers to the reaction in the photosynthesis that takes place in the absence of light.

Darwin's theory

Proposed by Charles Darwin in *On Origin of Species*, the theory relates to the origin of species and evolution by natural selection and inheritance of successful variation.

Database

The term refers to a well-organised collection of data in a computer to be extracted as and when desired conveniently.

Data compression

It means reducing the size of data with the help of shorter codes, variable bit length, etc.

Dating techniques

It is a scientific method used to determine the age of organic materials, such as rocks, archaeological sites, etc. Radioactive carbon C^{14} is used for this purpose. For example, a rock it is measured to find out how much of a rock's radioactive material has changed since its formation.

Davy lamp

Invented by Humphrey Davy in 1816, the lamp is used in mines to test the presence of poisonous gas which helps to prevent the explosions. It is a safety lamp which consists of a metal gauze that surrounds the flame and prevents ignition of gas outside the gauze.

DDT

Dichlorodiphenyltrichloroethane; it is an insecticide widely used to control pests or insects. It gets accumulate in soils, hence its use is now restricted

Death

It refers to the point when all processes stop functioning any longer that maintain life of an organism. In human beings, it is diagnosed by the permanent cessation of heartbeat.

Death rate

It is defined as the rate at which a particular species or population dies irrespective of the cause leading to their death. The death rate has a significant role in controlling the size of a population.

De Broglie, Louis-Victor Pierre Raymond (1892-1987)

He was a French Physicist who is widely known for his theory of wave-particle duality which proved very important in quantum theory. He was awarded Nobel Prize for this work in 1929.

De Broglie, Louis-Victor Pierre Raymond

Debye

In the electrostatic system, it is a unit of electric dipole moment. It has the 3.335 64 × 10^{-13} coulomb meter.

Deca- (*Symbol* da)

It is used as a prefix in the metric system to denote 10 times.

Decay

It is used for the following:

1. It denotes the breakdown of organic matter of dead plants and animals.
2. It refers to spontaneous transformation of one radioactive nuclide into a daughter nuclide.

Deci- (*Symbol* d)

It is a prefix used in the metric system to denote one-tenth.

Decibel

It is a unit used for comparing two power levels, usually the sound intensities or electrical signals. One decibel is equal to d0.1 bel. A whisper has an intensity of 20d, while one decibel represents an increase of some 26%, and it is the smallest change that human ear can detect.

Deciduous forests

The term is used for the forests in which plants and trees shed their leaves at the end of each growing season, usually in autumn in the temperate regions or in the dry season in tropics just to reduce transpiration.

Deciduous forests

Deciduous teeth

It is the first of the two sets of teeth in the mammals which is replaced by the permanent teeth.

Decimal system

It is a number system which is based on the number 10. It is the most commonly used system.

Decoction

It is a solution made by boiling plant materials in water which is later filtered for use.

Decomposer

The term is used for an organism which obtains energy from the dead organisms, or animals or plant wastes. Decomposers are mostly bacteria or fungi which cause their decay.

Deficiency disease

It refers to a disease which is cause by a deficiency of essential nutrient in food intake, mainly by vitamins, minerals, amino acids and other food factors. For example scurvy is caused by inadequacy of vitamin C, goitre by lack of iodine, and rickets by lack of vitamin D.

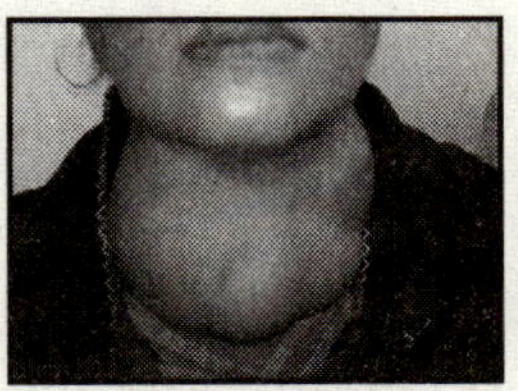

Deficiency disease

Deforestation

The term is used for a large-scale destruction of forests for various purposes such as for timber, fuel, etc. or to clear the land for farming or mining without planting new trees. Deforestation causes soil erosion, flood, drought, and a loss of wildlife since it is their natural habitat. Deforestation intensifies the greenhouse effect.

Degassing

It refers to the removal of dissolved, absorbed or adsorbed gases from a liquid or solid. Degassing is very important in vacuum system.

Degree

It is a unit of measurement of angle or arc. Temperature is measured in degrees. A circle is divided into 360°.

Dehydration

It refers to the following:

1. Removal of water.
2. A chemical reaction in which there is a loss of hydrogen and oxygen in a compound in a ratio of 2:1. For example, copper sulphate contains water and is blue in colour but when it dehydrate it becomes power and has no colour.
3. In Medicine, it means loss of water from animal body which sometimes is fatal unless it is replaced orally or intravenously.

Deliquescence

It refers to the phenomenon in which a substance absorbs water from the atmosphere and gets dissolved in it.

Dementia

It is a mental disorder marked by gradual memory loss, change in personality and impaired reasoning. Dementia can occur after the age of 60.

Dendrite

It denotes the following:

1. In Neurology, it refers to a nerve fibre of the cell body of a motor neuron which has many branches. It connects the axons of other neurons and transmits impulses from them to the cell body.

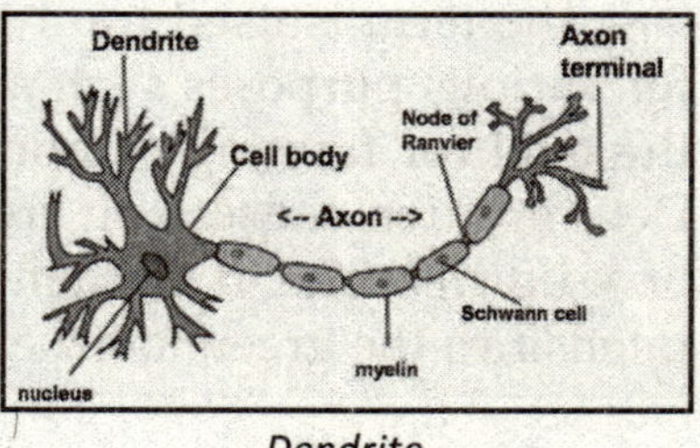

Dendrite

2. In Chemistry, a crystal which has branched in growth into two parts. Such crystals have tree-like appearance.

Dendrology

It is a branch of botany which deals with the classification and distribution of trees and other woody plants.

Dengue

It is a viral disease transmitted to man by the mosquitoes. Symptoms include fever, headache sore throat, rash, vomiting, bradycardia and depression. It is a tropical disease which is treated with analgesic, fluid transfusion, etc.

Densimeter

Also called gravitometer, it is an instrument used for measuring the density of a solid, liquid or gas.

Density

It refers to the mass per unit volume of a substance. Its SI unit is kg m^{-3}.

Dental formula

It is a representation of the dentition of an animal. A dental formula shows the number of different teeth in one half of the upper and lower jaw. The total number of teeth in both jaws is obtained by adding up all the numbers in the dental formula and multiplying them by 2.

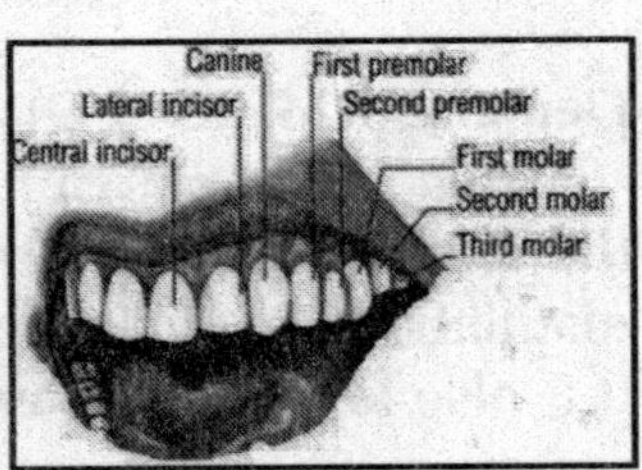

Dental formula

Dentition

It includes the type, number and arrangement of teeth in an animal.

Depleted uranium

The term is used for uranium mostly consisting of uranium-238. It is obtained as a by-product of enriching natural uranium or can be obtained from processing plant. It has high density.

Dermatitis

It refers to an inflammation of skin marked by small blisters, redness and itching. It is a type of eczema, caused by external agents.

Dermatology

It refers to the study of skin, its structure, function and diseases.

Desertification

The term can be defined as a gradual conversion of fertile land into desert usually as a result of human activities such as indiscriminate cutting of forest trees, overgrazing of livestock, overintensive cultivation of crop plants, especially monoculture, etc. It badly affects the ecological balance.

Detergent

It is a cleaning agent which when added to water improve its cleaning properties. Detergents are made from fats. Soaps are examples of detergent.

Deuterium (*Symbol* D)

It is an isotope of hydrogen which is present in water as the oxide HDO. It is obtained by electrolysis or fractional distillation. Its nucleus contains one neutron and one proton. It is also known as heavy hydrogen.

Dewar flask

It is a vessel used for storing hot or cold liquids at the same temperature. It consists of a double-walled glass vessel with vacuum in between the walls which keeps the transfer of heat from the surroundings to the minimum. The inner surface of the glass vessel is silvered to prevent the loss or gain of heat by radiation.

Dewar flask

Dew point

It refers to the temperature at which water vapour in the air is saturated. Below the dew point water vapour condenses to form droplets of water.

Dialysis

It is a process used for separating especially waste substances out of the blood of people suffering from acute or chronic kidney failure with the help of an artificial kidney.

Diamond

It is an allotropic form of pure carbon, crystallised under great pressure. It is transparent and colourless which has high melting point and hardness. It is the hardest known mineral used for cutting, grinding and polishing. Diamonds occur in kimberlite.

Diamond

Diaphragm

It is used for the following:

1. In anatomy, it is a membrane that separates the thorax and abdomen in mammals. It helps in respiration.
2. In optics, an opaque disc with circular aperture at its center used to control the total light flux passing through an optical system.

Diarrhoea

It is a medical condition in which excessive fluid is lost from the bowel because of an infection leading to dehydration. If the fluid loss is not replaced timely it can be fatal.

Diastole

It is the phase of heartbeat occurring between expansion and relaxation of heart when the heart muscles relax allowing the entry of blood from the veins into the heart.

Diathermy

It is a method of treatment in which high frequency electric discharge is passed on body tissues to relieve pain.

Diesel engine

It is internal combustion engine in which diesel or light weight fuel oil is used. It is a compression-ignition engine which does not require a spark plug as used in petrol engine.

Diffraction

It refers to a phenomenon in which waves spread or bend as they pass through an aperture. It has a significant role in the propagation of radio wave over the curved surface of the earth. The phenomenon contributed to the wave theory of light.

Diffusion

It denotes the following:

1. The scattering of a beam of light by reflection or by transmission.
2. The spread of molecules of a material through a solid, liquid or gas because of the random kinetic movement of the molecules. Diffusion is quick in solids and gases but it is very slow in solids. Diffusion helps in absorption in plant and animal cells.

Digestion

It is the process by which the ingested food is broken down in an organism into a chemically simpler form to be absorbed and assimilated with the help of digestive juices in different parts of alimentary canal.

Digestive system

It includes the organs involved in the process of digestion of food which is comprised of alimentary canal and teeth, tongue, liver, pancreas and gall bladder.

Digestive system

Digital recording

It refers to a method of recording or transmitting sound in which the sound itself is not transmitted or recorded instead sound wave is treated differently and then it is recorded and transmitted. This method is used for high quality recording.

Dilation

It means a change or increase in volume especially because of the stretching and expansion of blood vessels.

Dilute

It is a solution which has a relatively low concentration of solute.

Dinosaur

It belongs to an extinct terrestrial reptile constituting the dominant land animal in the Jurassic and Cretaceous periods, some 190 to 60 million years ago.

Dinosaur

Dipole

It is used for the following:

1. It refers to an uneven distribution of magnetic or electrical characteristics within a molecule or substance in a way that it has two equal but opposite charges. Dipoles are electrical and magnetic. Its SI unit is the coulomb meter.
2. An aerial commonly used for frequencies below 30 megahertz, though there are some above this frequency in use.

Direct current (DC)

It refers to an electric current in which the net flow of charge is in one direction only unlike the alternating current (AC).

Disinfectant

It is a chemical agent which kills or prohibits the growth of disease-producing microorganisms and is toxic to living tissues. Examples of disinfectant are bleaching powder, cresol and phenol.

Dispersal

It means spread of offspring of plants and animals.

Dispersal helps in the survival of animals by reducing competition between parents and offspring. Wind, water and animals are the agents of dispersal.

Displacement

It refers to the following:

1. It is a chemical reaction in which one element or group of elements take the place of another.
2. It is defined as the amount of fluid displaced by a floating or submerged body, e.g. ship.

Distillation

It is a process of boiling a liquid, condensing and finally collecting the vapour. The liquid thus collected is called distillate. The process is used for separating pure liquid from its mixture.

Diuretic

It refers to a substance or any other agent that increases the rate of urine formation leading to the increased rate of loss of salts from the body. Diuretics are used for the treatment of oedema, hypertension, etc.

Diverging lens

The term is used for the lens which can refract or reflect a parallel beam of light passing through it to spread instead of focussing it to a point unlike converging lens.

DNA (Deoxyribonucleic acid)

It is the genetic material of most organisms containing genetic information in coded form. It plays a significant role in determination of hereditary characteristics. It is a spiral-shaped ladder-like double stranded nucleic acid linked together by hydrogen bonds between specific complementary bases.

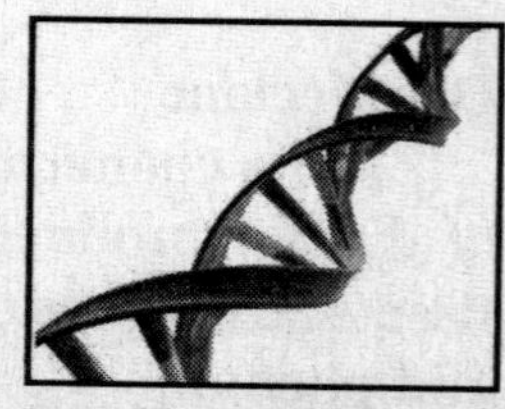

DNA (Deoxyribonucleic acid)

DNA replication

It is a process by which DNA makes exact copies of itself. It is controlled by enzyme DNA polymerase.

Doppler effect

The term is used for the apparent change in the frequency of wave motion of sound or electromagnetic radiation resulting from the relative motion between the source and the observer. For example, the observed change in the pitch of the whistle of a train as it approaches and then it fades away. Other example of Doppler effect is the red shift of light from distant star. It is named after the Austrian physicist Christian Doppler (1803-53) who suggested it in his attempt to explain the colouration of stars.

Dormancy

It refers to an inactive period in the life of an animal or plant during which metabolism is reduced. It helps them to survive under unfavourable condition. For example hibernation and aestivation in animal help them to survive the extreme of cold and heat respectively.

Dormancy

Dosimeter

It is a device used for measuring the radiation received by a person working with radioactive material or X-ray.

Down's syndrome

It is a congenital form of mental retardation caused by chromosome abnormality in which there are three copies of chromosome 21, instead of the two. It is marked by broad face and slanted eyes, short fingers, and weak muscles.

Drug

It refers to any chemical substance used for the prevention, diagnosis and cure of a disease, e.g. antibiotics, analgesics, anaesthetics, antihistamines, etc. Sometimes drugs are taken just for pleasure they induce, for example narcotics, amphetamine and tranquilizers.

Dry ice

The term is used for dry carbon dioxide which is used as a refrigerant. It has a temperature of −79°C and is used to preserve food stuff. Dry ice sublimes from solid state to gas rather than melting.

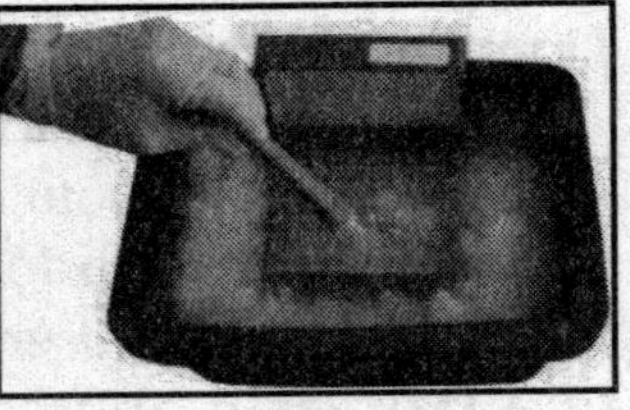

Dry ice

Drying oil

It refers to natural oil, e.g. linseed oil which hardens when exposed to air. It is used for paints and varnishes.

Ductility

The term is used to denote the ability of some metals, e.g. copper, which can retain their strength when their shape is changed. Such metals can be drawn to thin wires without being cracked or broken.

Ductless glands

The term refers to glands which produce hormones and secretes them directly into the bloodstream. Thyroid, pituitary, adrenal, etc. are examples of ductless glands.

Dumas' method

It is used for the following:

1. It is a method of finding out the amount of nitrogen in an organic compound.
2. It refers to the method of finding the relative molecular masses of volatile liquids by weighing. It is named after the French Chemist, J.B.S. Dumas.

Duodenum

It is the beginning part of small intestine in vertebrates. It is the site where the action of bile, pancreatic juices, and the enzymes secreted by the digestive glands is effected as a process of digestion of food.

Duralumin

It is a trade name for a class of lightweight aluminium alloys containing copper, magnesium, manganese, often silicon. Because of strength and lightweight duralumin is extensively used in aircraft and racing cars.

Dura meter

It is the outermost covering of the brain in vertebrates. It is also the toughest part surrounding the delicate inner meninges.

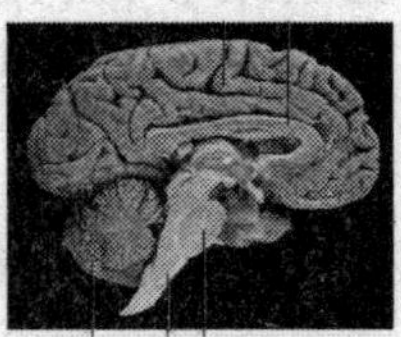

Dura meter

Dutch metal

The term is used for an alloy of zinc and copper which can be made into thin sheets. It is used in jewellery.

Dwarfism

It is used to refer the physical abnormality in which human body fails to gain normal growth because of hormone deficiency.

Dwarf planet

The term is used for small solar body which directly orbits the sun and not the other planet. It has sufficient mass to have contracted to a spherical shape. So far five objects have been classified as dwarf planets which include Pluto.

Dyes

They are substances which impart colour to leather, textile, papers, etc. usually organic compounds are used for dyeing.

Dynamics

It is the branch of mechanics which deals with the motion of bodies under the action of force, including time intervals, distances and masses.

Dynamite

The term refers to nitroglycerin based high explosives, which is used for blasting. It was invented by Alfred Nobel, the founder of the Nobel prize, in 1867.

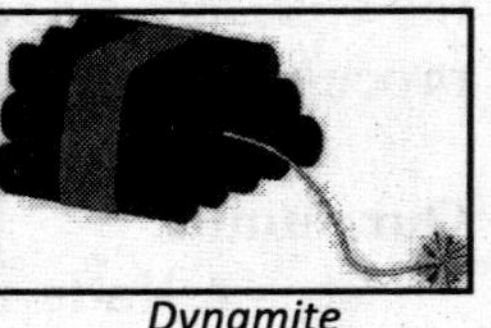

Dynamite

Dynamo

It is a device which converts mechanical energy into electrical energy. A dynamo consists of a large field magnet with a coil rotating in the magnet field.

Dynamometer

It is an instrument used for measuring power.

Dyne

It is a unit of force in the CGS system. It is the force required to give a mass of one gram an acceleration of 1 cm per second^{-2}; 1 dyne = 10^{-5} newton.

Dysentery

The term is used to refer the inflammation of the bowels leading to frequent discharge of mucus, blood and faeces. It is caused by infection.

Dyspepsia

It is a medical condition in which there is pain caused by difficulty in digestion. It can be relieved a by a carminative dose

Dystrophy

It refers to a medical condition in which an organ usually muscles get defective nutrition. Some people are born with the condition in which muscles gradually become weaker. It has a genetic background.

❑

E

It refers to the following:

1. In physics, it is the symbol for emissivity.
2. It is the abbreviation for erythrocyte

Ear

It is the sense organ of hearing and balance in the vertebrates which is divided into the outer ear and middle ear. The outer ear collects and transmits sound waves and the inner ear contains the organs which maintain the balance.

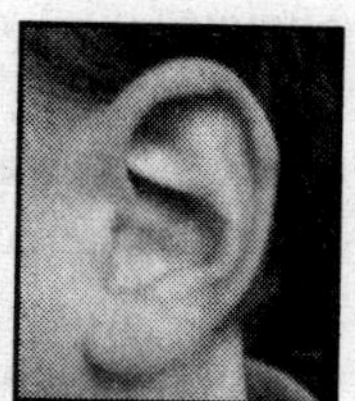

Ear

Ear ossicles

The term is used for the part of ear which consists of three small bones — the incus, malleus, and stapes — forming the part of the middle ear.

Earth

It is one of the nine planets of the solar system which orbit the sun which has spherical shape and is flattened at the poles. It is at a mean distance from the sun of 149600000 km with an equatorial diameter of 12,756 km. The earth rotates about its axis once in 23 hours 56 minutes and 4 seconds. About 70% of the total area of the earth is covered with water. The earth consists of three layers of which the gaseous layer is called atmosphere, the liquid hydrosphere and the solid lithosphere. The solid part of the earth consists of crust, mantle and core.

The core is the uppermost layer; the mantle is the middle layer next to crust and the core is the innermost part of the earth which is believed to be liquid.

Earthquake

Earthquake

The term is used for a series of shock resulting from a sudden movement or shaking of the earth's crust caused by volcanic eruption or displacement along fault lines. The shock or tremor may range from mild to large scale movement. The point from where the tremor originates is called seismic focus, and the point just there above the ground is called epicentre. The magnitude of the earthquake is measured on the Richter scale.

Earth science

The term is used for a group of sciences, namely geology, oceanography, geography, meteorology, geochemistry, geophysics which concerned with the study of earth including its structure, age and other aspects.

Ebonite

Also called vulcanite, it is a hard insulating material made by the volcanisation of rubber with sulphur.

Ecdysis (moulting)

It used for the following:

1. The periodic shedding of the outer layer of the epidermis of reptiles which help in their growth.
2. The loss of outer cuticle in arthropods.

Echo

It refers to the repetition of a sound wave by reflection from an object or surface. The delay between the two indicates the distance between the object and the reflecting surface.

Echo sounder

It is an apparatus used to find out the depth of water under a ship. It also helps in locating the shipwrecks and submarines.

Eclampsia

It is a medical condition affecting a woman during pregnancy or after childbirth with symptoms of convulsion and coma accompanied with high blood pressure and oedema. It is caused by blood poisoning during the pregnancy.

Eclipse

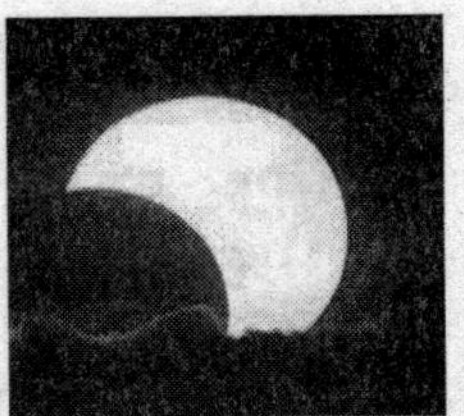

It is used to refer the obstruction of light from a celestial body during its passage behind or through the shadow of another body. In solar eclipse, the sun, moon and earth are aligned in a way that the moon obstructs the light from the sun and casts its shadow on the earth. The sun becomes partially or wholly invisible. In lunar eclipse, the earth casts its shadow on the moon and the moon becomes partially or wholly eclipsed. In total eclipse, light is completely obstructed while in partial eclipse the light is only partially obstructed.

Ecology

It deals with the relationship of plants and animals with their natural environment, including both living and non-living.

Ecosystem

The term broadly includes the entire community of living things including producers, consumers and decomposers with their interaction with one another. Organisms are classified on the basis of their position in an ecosystem.

Ectoparasite

It refers to a parasite which lives on the host's body unlike the endoparasite which lives inside the host's.

Eczema

It is a skin disease which affects the epidermis. Symptoms include red rashes, itching, small blisters, thickening and scaling of skin, etc. Eczema may be acute or chronic.

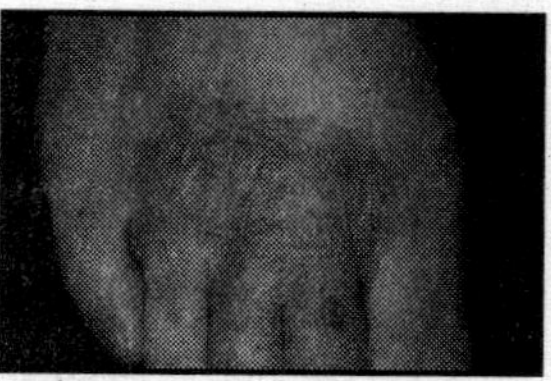

Eczema

Eddy current

The term is used for induced electric current in a changing magnetic field or other electrical appliances which causes a loss of useful energy. It is therefore metal cores are made of insulated sheets of metal to reduce the wastage of this energy.

Effector

The term includes cell or organ which responds when stimulated by a cell nerve. Muscles and glands are examples of effector which bring about change or effect in the function of the body.

Effervescence

It refers to the production of bubbles in a liquid usually caused by chemical reaction.

Efficiency

The term is used to describe the performance of a machine or engine which is actually the ratio of the output to the input of a machine expressed in percentage. Generally, the efficiency of a machine varies depending on the condition under which it operates. Usually, it operates with highest efficiency at a load.

Effusion

It refers to the flow of gas through a small aperture, usually from a region of high pressure to low pressure.

Egestion

It means the expulsion of waste materials particularly undigested food materials from the body through anus.

Egg

It denotes the following:

1. It is used for fertilized zygote in egg-lying animals, for example birds and insects. Eggs are protected by egg membrane.
2. In plants and animals, it refers to the mature female reproductive cell.

Einstein, Albert

He was a US Physicist who was born in Germany and later took Swiss nationality in 1901. His rose to fame with the publication of papers on Brownian movement, photoelectric effect, energy and inertia and special theory of relativity. In 1915 he published the general theory of relativity related to gravitation. In 1921, he was awarded the Nobel Prize for Physics.

Einstein, Albert

Einstein equation

Also called the mass energy equation, it was announced by Einstein in 1905 which came to be known as $E = mc^2$, where E is the quantity of energy, m is mass, and c is the speed of light.

Elasticity

It refers to the property of certain materials that enables them to get back the original form and dimension when the applied force has been removed. There is no distortion when the force is removed. The material gets stretched when the applied force is great and it has reached the elastic limit.

Elastomer

It is a natural or synthetic rubber which can be deformed under the influence of a force and resume its original shape when the applied force is removed.

Electrical energy

It is a form of energy produced by the electrical charges as a result of their position in an electric or magnetic field. It is given by the formula *Q*, *V* where *Q* represents electrical charge of the body and *V* represents electrical energy.

Electric bell

It is a device in which an electromagnetically operated hammer strikes a bell, causing electric current to flow. The flow produces a magnetic field attracting an iron armature that produces sound.

Electricity

It is a form of energy produced as a result of electric charges and their effects, either moving or stationary.

Electric lighting

The term is used for light or illumination produced by electric currents, e.g. the arc lamp, the light bulb, fluorescent tube, etc.

Electric motor

It is a machine used for converting electrical energy into mechanical energy. An electric motor works on the principle that a current passing through a coil within a magnetic field experiences forces that can be used to rotate the coil.

Electric motor

Electric organ

It is an organ found in certain fish, e.g. electric ray and electric eel. It gives an electric shock when touched. It is used as defence mechanism against prey and predators. In some species, this organ is used to produce a weak electric field in the surrounding to ensure safe navigation there.

Electrocardiogram (ECG)

It is actually a graph obtained by recordings of the electrical activity of the heart. A change in the normal pattern of the

ECG indicates abnormality in the functioning of the heart. ECG is of great value in the diagnosis of heart disease.

Electrochemistry

It is a branch of chemistry which studies chemical properties and reaction, including electrical cells and electrolysis.

Electrodialysis

It refers to a method used for obtaining pure water from water containing salt. The water is fed into a cell for purification, which has two electrodes in it. After the process the fed water is separated into two streams – one of pure water and the other of more concentrated solution.

Electrodialysis

Electrodynamics

It concerns the study of relationship between electric and magnetic forces, their causes and effects and the relationship between them.

Electrodynamometer

It is an instrument used for measuring voltage, current and power in DC and AC circuits

Electroencephalogram (EEG)

It is a graphical recording of the electrical activity of the brain through. It is done with the help of electrodes, attached to the head on a strip of paper. Encephalogram is of great help in detecting brain disorders such as tumours, epilepsy, or brain damage. The pattern of EEG reflects the brain activity.

Electrolysis

The term is used for the chemical reaction caused by flow of current through an electrolyte. In electrolysis positive ions migrate to the cathode and negative ions to the anode. For example-in electrolysis of water, oxygen is obtained at the anode while hydrogen at the cathode.

Electrolyte

It is used for a substance which when dissolved in water or in molten substance conducts electric current during electrolysis. Strong electrolytes, for example acids and alkalis, and many soluble salts produce many ions. In electrolysis, ions are the carrier of currents and not the electrons.

Electrolytic cell

It is a cell or a vessel in which electrolysis takes place. It is in it the current is passed through the electrolyte from an external source.

Electrolytic corrosion

It refers to a corrosion which occurs as a result of electrochemical reaction.

Electrolytic gas

The term is used for the highly explosive gas produced by the electrolysis of water. It contains hydrogen and oxygen in 2:1.

Electrolytic rectifier

It refers to a rectifier which has two electrodes, immersed in an electrolyte. It is used to convert an alternating current into direct current. The current can be made to pass in one direction only by suitably choosing electrodes and electrolyte.

Electromagnet

It refers to a soft ferromagnetic core which has a coil of insulated wire around it. The core get magnetised when the current flows in the coil and magnetism is lost when the current stops. Electromagnets have many applications such as in switches, solenoids, cranes, lifting metals, etc.

Electromagnet

Electromagnetic induction

In Physics, it means the production of an electromotive force in a conductor, by magnets and magnetic fields. It is done through the motion of a conductor in a magnetic field cutting magnetic lines of force or changing the magnetic field.

Electromagnetism

It is the branch of physics which studies magnetic forces produced by electricity or the electric effects produced by the magnetic fields.

Electrometallurgy

It deals with the uses of electrical processes in the separation of metals from their ores, the refining of metals and forming of metals.

Electrometer

It is an instrument used for measuring a voltage difference without drawing considerable current from the source. Electrometers are also used to measure low currents by passing the current through a high resistance.

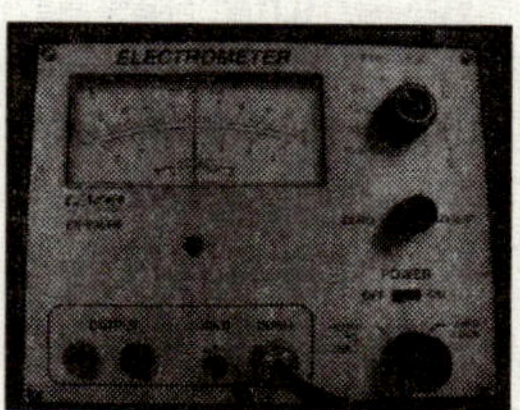

Electrometer

Electromotive force (e.m.f.)

The term is used for the driving force or generator or its potential difference in open circuit when no current is flowing through the cell. The unit of e.m.f. is volt.

Electron

It is the fundamental and one of the three basic particles in an atom with a negative charge. Electrons are present in all atoms in groupings called shells around the nucleus. The number of electrons equals the number of protons.

Electron configuration

The term can be defined as the arrangement of electrons around the nucleus of an atom. The electron configuration of nitrogen is 2, 5 which means that the first shell has 2 electrons while in the second shell there are 5 electrons.

Electron gun

It is a device used for producing a steady beam of electrons in cathode ray tubes and electron microscopes, etc. It has a grid which controls the number of electrons emitted from the heated cathode.

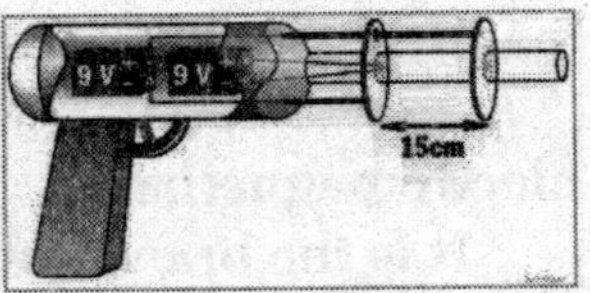

Electron gun

Electronic mail

It refers to a system of sending and receiving messages, documents, etc. through the network of computers. The senders and the receivers may be situated worldwide and they do not need to be at their computers at the same time to communicate. The sender has to have an email by means of a mail-sending computer programme, and a mail transport system then takes the responsibility to deliver the mail to the address indicated in the mail.

Electronics

The term is used for the study and design of control, communication, and computing devices where the motion of electrons is controlled, including the development of semiconductors, thermionic valves and allied devices.

Electron lens

It is a device used to focus an electron beam, analogous to an optical lens. It contains a coil or coils which produces a magnetic field or an arrangement to produce an electric field. Electron lenses are used in electron microscopes and cathode ray tubes.

Electron microscope

It is a microscope which uses a beam of electrons to produce a magnified image of a small object. It is a high resolution microscopes which uses electrons instead of light.

Electroplating

Electroplating

It refers to a process in which one metal is coated with a thin layer of another metal by electrolysis, largely to protect it from corrosion or often for decoration as well. For example, iron can be electroplated with nickel or chromium.

Electroscope

It is an instrument used for detecting electrical potential difference.

Electrostatics

The term is used for the study of electric charges at rest, the forces between them including the electric fields involved.

Element

It refers to a substance which cannot be split into simpler substance. An element consists of entirely of atoms of the same number. There are 92 naturally occurring elements. Elements are categorised as metals and non-metals.

Elephantiasis

It is used for a medical condition which has symptoms like swelling and inflammation of limbs, particularly legs which is caused by obstruction in the flow of lymph. Elephantiasis is spread by mosquitoes.

Eliminator

It is a device which is used as a substitute for batteries. It consists of a rectifier used with an alternating current.

El Nino

The term is used to refer the phenomenon characterised by a surge of warm water eastward towards the west coast of South America, mainly in the Peru Current. It occurs every few years largely in the equatorial part of the Pacific Ocean.

The phenomenon has great effects on the local climate. Besides, it has wider effects on the climate all across the world.

Elton, Charles Southerland (1900-91)

He was a British Zoologist and Ecologist who studied population fluctuations. He was the first Zoologist to study animals in relation to their environment. He is credited to have found the Bureau of Animal Population at Oxford in 1932. He explored the nature of food chains.

Embryo

It refers to the early development stage of an a plant or an animal or a human being.

Embryology

It is the branch of science which studies the development the early stage of life, i.e. fertilized egg and the new adult organism. It is limited to the period between fertilization of the egg to birth of the new one.

Emerald

It is one of the highly prized gemstones and a variety of beryl. It is found in the Muzo mines in Colombia, besides South Africa and India.

Emetic

The term is used for a substance that causes vomiting.

Emu

It is a flightless bird found in Australia. Emu does not have a head crest like cassowary.

Emu

Emulsion

The term refers to a mixture of two or more immersible liquids held in suspension. Usually, emulsions involve a dispersion of water in an oil and or a dispersion of oil in water which are stabilized by an emulsifier, e.g. detergents.

Enamel

It is used for the following:

1. In zoology, refers to the hard material formed over the crown of a tooth. It is smooth, white and is highly rich in minerals containing calcium.

2. In chemistry, it is a finely powdered oil paint which has shining property.

Encephalitis

It is a medical condition characterised by inflammation in the brain. It is caused by bacteria or virus. Bacterial encephalitis is endemic in some parts of the world.

Endemic

It is used for a disease or pest persistent in an area. For example-malaria is endemic in tropical region, i.e. South Africa.

Endocarp

It refers to the inner hard stony coat covering a seed, as in many drupes, e.g. coconut.

Endocrine glands

The term is used for the glands in animals which produce hormones and secrete them directly into the bloodstream. Endocrine glands include pituitary, thyroid, adrenal, parathyroid glands, part of the pancreas, ovary and testis. Endocrine glands control various activities in the body such as growth and sexual development.

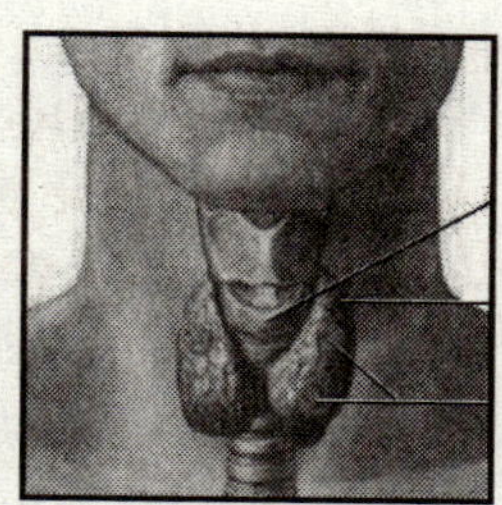

Endocrine glands

Endocrinology

The term is used for the study of the endocrine glands, including their structure, function and the hormones they produce.

End organ

The term broadly includes the muscle end plate at the end

of a motor neuron and the receptor at the end of a sensory neuron. In other words, it is the structure at the end of a peripheral nerve.

Endorphin

It is used for the peptides or polypeptides neurotransmitter produced by the pituitary gland and hypothalamus in vertebrates. It has pain-relieving effects like morphine.

Endoscopy

The term is used for the direct examination of the internal organs of the body with the help of an instrument called endoscope, which has a camera and light source. The patient has to swallow it for an abdominal examination. It is flexible.

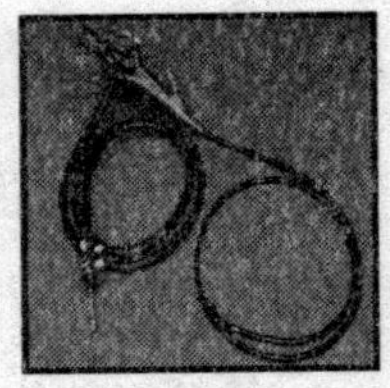

Endoscopy

Endoskeleton

It is an internal supporting structure in vertebrates, like the bony structure. It consists of bones and cartilage and gives shape to the body and protects the vital organs like brain, heart and lungs.

End plate

It refers to the area of the plasma membrane of a muscle cell situated just beneath the motor nerve. At the end plate the release of a neurotransmitter induces contraction of the muscle fibre.

End point

It denotes the point or the final stage when the chemical reaction is complete.

Energy

The term is used to refer the capacity of a system or machine to work. Like work itself, the unit of energy is joule. Energy can be classified into two category - kinetic and potential energy. However, there are other forms of energy, e.g. heat, light, electrical, chemical, sound, wave, etc.

Engine

It is a device which converts one form of energy into other, e.g. mechanical work.

Engine

Entomology

It is the branch of Zoology which studied insects.

Entropy (*Symbol* S)

It is a measure of the disorder of a system, molecular, atomic or ionic. The higher the entropy the greater the disorder. Its unit is joules per mole per degree($1mol^{-1}K^{-1}$).

Environment

It refers to the physical, biological and chemical conditions of a region in which a plant, organism or animal lives. It includes the whole surroundings.

Enzyme

It is a protein which speeds up the rate of a biochemical reaction. It is a complex organism which is influenced by substrate concentration and by temperature and pH.

Epidemic

It is an infectious disease which affects a large number of people in an area, e.g. cholera and influenza.

Epidemiology

It is used for the scientific study of diseases which affects a large number of people largely with the aim of finding measures to control them. Traditionally it was focused to the study of only infectious diseases like influenza, typhoid but today it also covers non-infectious diseases like heart disease, diabetes, etc.

Epiglottis

It is a flap of cartilage in mammals which closes the glottis when food is swallowed thus preventing it from entering into the trachea. It is attached to the wall of the pharynx near the tongue.

Epilepsy

It is a hereditary disease which affects the brain. It is characterised by fits accompanied with loss of consciousness and tremor. Barbiturates are used to control the disease.

Epsom salt

It is hydrated magnesium sulphate which is used in textile and leather industry. It is also used as laxative in medicine.

Equator

It is an imaginary line which divides the earth into two equals—the northern and the southern hemisphere. It is equidistant from the two geographical poles.

Equator

Equilibrium

The term can be defined as a state of a system in which reactions, forces and influences are balanced out and there is no net change. Equilibriums are of different kinds—stable equilibrium, unstable equilibrium, dynamic equilibrium and thermal equilibrium.

Ergocalciferol

It is a fat-soluble vitamin found in yeast. It is formed by ultraviolet light. Fish liver oil is the major dietary source of it. It is also called vitamin D_2.

Ergosterol

It is a sterol present in bacteria, fungi, algae and plants which is converted into vitamin D_2 by the ultraviolet light.

Erosion

It implies the destruction of land surface by various natural agents like rivers, wind, ocean waves, ice, etc.

Erythrocytes

The term is used for the red blood cells which contains the red pigment haemoglobin. It transports oxygen to various parts of the body. In mammals they are disc-shaped. In man one cubic millimetre blood contains 4.5 to 5.5 million erythrocytes.

Essential amino acid

It is an amino acid that an organism is unable to synthesise in required quantities; hence it must be present in the diet. In humans the essential amino acids are: valine, leucine, methionine, histidine, threonine, lysine, isoleucine, phenylalanine, and tryptophan. These are required to synthesise protein and their deficiency leads to abnormality in growth and other problems.

Essential oil

The term is used for natural oil, e.g. citrus oils, flower oils, which has special scents secreted by the glands of some aromatic plants. Essential oils are extracted by steam distillation, extraction with cold neutral fats. Essential oils are used in perfumes, flavourings, and medicine.

Essential oil

Esters

These are organic compounds produced by the reaction between acids and alcohols. Esters are used as flavouring agents in the food industry. The process by which ester is produced is called esterification.

Estrogen

It is a hormone produced by the ovary in a woman. The hormone has a significant role in stimulating the growth of secondary sexual characteristics.

Ethanal

It is a colourless highly flammable liquid aldehyde, made from ethane. It is used as a starting material for making many organic compounds. It is used as a drug for inducing sleep. It is also used as a solid fuel in portable stoves. Its melting point is −121°C and boiling point is 20.8°C.

Ethanol

It is a colourless water soluble alcohol and an active agent used in intoxicating drinks. It is produced by fermentation of sugars using yeasts. Ethanol is used as a solvent. Its boiling point is 78.3°C and melting point is −114°C.

Ethanol

Ethers

The term includes organic compounds containing -O- in the molecules, e.g. dimethyl ether and diethyl ether, which are volatile and highly flammable compounds. They are made dehydrating alcohols using sulphuric acids.

Ethology

It refers to the study of animal behaviour in context of their natural surroundings. It includes the stimuli that are important in nature and how they influence their behaviour.

Eudiometer

It is an instrument used for measuring the changes in the volume of gases during chemical reaction.

Eugenics

The term relates to the study of methods improving the quality of human population with the help of genetic principles. Eugenics can be categorised as positive eugenics and negative eugenics. Positive eugenics prefers selective breeding enforced by law while negative eugenics focuses to elimination of harmful genes by counselling the prospective carriers.

Europium

It is a soft silvery-white metallic element of lanthanoids with boiling point 1597°C and melting point 822°C.it occurs in bastanite and monazite. It is widely used in television screen.

Eutectic

It refers to a solution or alloy with the lowest possible melting point.

Euthanasia

The term is used for an act of intentionally ending life of an animal or person to relieve further suffering, incurable or painful disease. It can be done by administering a lethal drug or by withholding vital treatment. Euthanasia is a controversial issue and is illegal in most of the countries.

Evaporation

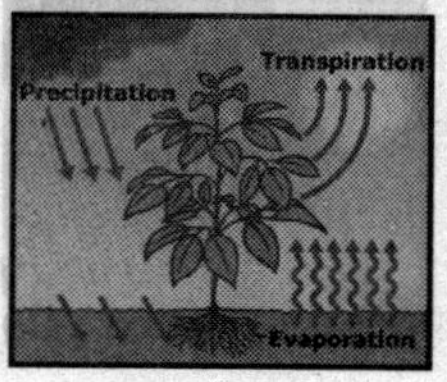

It is a process which changes a liquid into vapour at temperature below the boiling point of the liquid.

Evergreen plants

The term is used for the plants which are green round the year and they do not shed their leaves.

Excretion

It refers to the elimination of waste materials, e.g. water, urine, uric acid, carbon dioxide, etc., by an organism produced as a result of metabolic activity. In plants and simple animals, waste materials are excreted by simple diffusion while in higher animals there are special organs or system to do this.

Exfoliation

It denotes the erosion in rocks resulting from weathering. Basalt and granite are the commonly affected rock forms. Exfoliation is thought to be mainly caused by the variation in day-night temperature.

Exocrine glands

It is used for the glands which secretes through canals or ducts into a body cavity, e.g. sweat glands, mammary glands, etc.

Exosphere

It refers to the outermost layer of the earth's atmosphere which is about 400 km high. It is beyond the ionosphere.

Expectorant

It is a substance or medicine which helps in removing secretion from the lungs or respiratory tract.

Expiration

It is a process by which air or water vapour is given out of the respiratory organs. It constitutes a part of respiration.

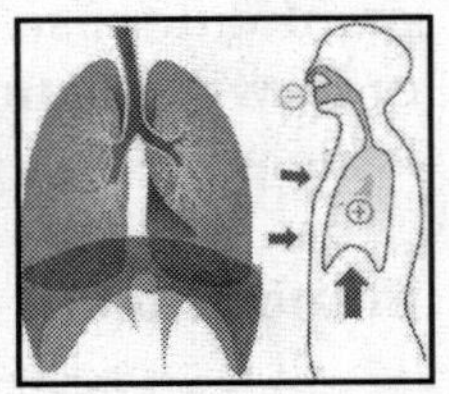

Expiration

Explosive

The term refers to a substance which causes explosion as a result of chemical reaction when ignited or denoted. A large amount of gas and heat accompanied by light, sound and shock wave are produced as a result of chemical reaction. Examples of explosives are dynamite, nitroglycerine, trinitrotoluene, etc.

Extensor

It is a muscle that helps a limb to extend or straighten, e.g. biceps, triceps, etc.

Extinction

The term implies a total disappearance of a species from the earth due to various factors such as destruction of habitats or overexploitation of species which are hunted. Extinction can be local or global. Today, dinosaurs are no more there on the earth because they are extinct.

Eye

It is the organ of sight in animals. Insects have compound eyes while most animals have simple eye which has acomplex structure. Normally, eyes are spherical. Human eyes mainly consist of parts, namely cornea, pupil, retina, aqueous humour, vitreous humour, and opic nerve. Light gets refracted by the cornea and images are formed onto the retina.

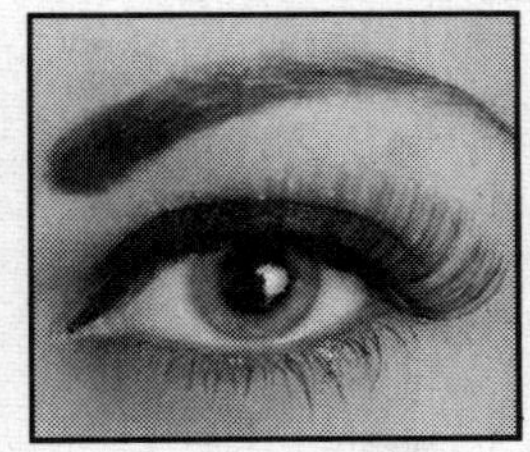

Eye

Eyepiece

It is the lens or lens system in an optical instrument which usually produces a magnified image of the image previously formed by the instrument. An observer sees the object through eyepiece.

Factor VIII

It is one of the blood clotting factors which is a soluble protein. Its deficiency or defects causes the fatal disease haemophilia in which blood does not clot.

Facultative

The term is used for the organisms which can survive in different habitats, for example - anaerobic bacteria can live under anaerobic or aerobic conditions.

Faeces

It is used for the undigested waste material eliminated from the alimentary canal and bacteria and dead cells shed from the gut.

Fahrenheit scale

It is a temperature scale formerly used to measure human body temperature. In this scale, the melting point of ice is 32 degrees and boiling point of water is 212 degrees. The scale is no longer in scientific use. A temperature can be converted to the Celsius scale with the help of following formula:

$$C = 5\,(F - 32)/9$$

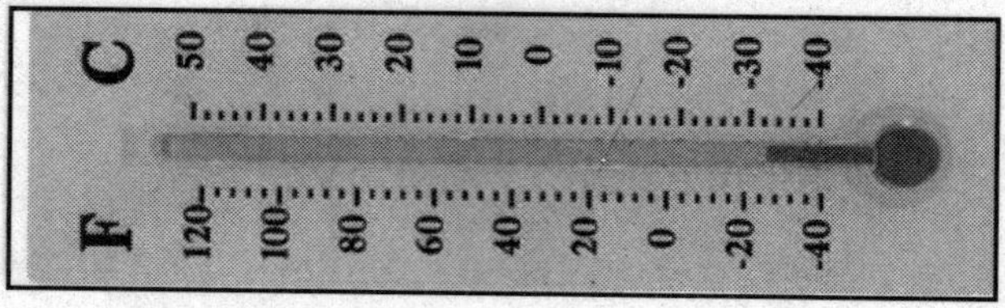

Fallopian tube

It is a pair of muscular tube through which egg cells are carried from the ovary to the womb. It is named after the Italian Anatomist Gabriel Fallopius.

Fallout

It denotes the following:

1. It refers to a radioactive particles produced from a nuclear explosion, e.g. nuclear bomb, hydrogen bomb or from nuclear reactor These particles are very harmful for human, plants and animals as well.
2. The term is also used for harmful chemicals released from factories.

False fruit

It refers to a fruit which is not formed by the ovary of the flower instead from the other parts, e.g. cashew nut.

False fruit

Fang

It is the root of a tooth in a carnivore. The poison tooth of a snake is also called fang.

Farad (*Symbol* F)

It is the SI unit of capacitance. The farad is a too big unit for most application; hence a practical unit is a smaller one called micro farad (10^{-6}F). The unit is named after great Scientist Michael Faraday.

Faraday cage

The term is used for an earthed screen which surrounds an electrical device so as to protect it from external electrical fields. It is made of metal wire.

Fast breeder

It is a nuclear reactor in which enriched uranium is used as fuel and a moderator is used to control the production of neutrons. A fast breeder produces the same fissile material as it uses.

Fast reactor

The term is used for a fast breeder reactor where neutrons lead to fission chain reaction. In a fast reactor uranium carbide is used to surround the core which is converted into plutonium and can be used again as fuel.

Fat

It is a mixture of lipids, solid at normal body temperature. It widely occurs in plants and animals and is a good source of their energy. The calorific value of fat is twice that of carbohydrates. Fats mainly consist of glycerides or ester of glycerol.

Fathom

It is a unit of measuring depth of water. One fathom is equal to 6 feet (1.83 m).

Fatigue

The term denotes a declining response of tissues, cells, etc. to stimulus applied. Usually, this happens after a continued stimulation of the structures.

Fatty acids

It refers to a monobasic organic compound consisting of a hydrocarbon chain and a terminal carboxyl group. Fatty acids are of two types – saturated or unsaturated.

Fault

It is a crack or fracture in earth's crust mainly caused by strains in rock leading to earthquakes.

Fault

Fauna

The term broadly includes all the animals present in a given habitat at certain point of time.

Fax

It is an abbreviated form of facsimile transmission or telefax. It is a system of transmission of data with the help of a fax machine.

Fax

Fecundity

It can be defined as the rate of fertility of the female species of an organism in a given time. Darwin's Theory of evolution by natural selection is based on fecundity.

Feldspar

It is a group of silicate minerals abundantly found in the earth's crust. Feldspar contains calcium, potassium, aluminium, sodium or barium.

Femur

It refers to the thigh bone in the vertebrates which articulates with the pelvic girdle and the other end with the tibia.

Fermentation

It can be defined as a series of biochemical changes in sugar solution caused by certain microorganisms, e.g. yeast, which leads to the formation of alcohol and carbon dioxide. It is a form of anaerobic respiration in microorganisms. Baking industry and brewery are based on fermentation.

Fermi

It is a unit of length equal to the length of 10^{-15} m. Formerly, it was used in nuclear physics. It is named after the eminent Scientist Enrico Fermi.

Fermi, Enrico (1901-54)

He was an Italian Physicist who later became US citizen and discovered the method to produce slow neutrons in 1934. He created new radioisotopes with the help of his discovery for which he was awarded the Nobel Prize in 1938. In 1942, he built the Fermi nuclear reactor in Chicago.

Fermium (*Symbol* Fm)

It is a radioactive transuranic metallic element. It belongs to actinoids; it has atomic weight 257; atomic no 100; melting point 1800k. It was first identified in 1952 from the first hydrogen bomb explosion.

Ferroalloys

The term refers to alloys of iron which contain high proportion of metal ore such as silicon, manganese, chromium and molybdenum. They are very useful for making alloy steels.

Fertility

It refers to the capability of an organism to reproduce. Plants and animals which produce sexually, fertility implies the number of fertilized eggs produced in a given time. In terms of plants, it denotes the relative capability of plants to support plant growth.

Fertilisation

It means fusion of male and female gametes or sex cells to form zygote with the genetic material of the parents. In self-fertilization, the male and female gametes come from the same individual while in cross-fertilization the gametes are derived from different individuals.

Fertilizer

It is a substance which is added to soil to increase its fertility. Fertilizers can be natural, e.g. composts, or synthetic chemicals such as nitrates and phosphates.

Fertilizer

Fetus

It is the embryo of a mammal particularly a human, after the eight week of development, when main features of an adult are recognisable.

Fibreglass

It is a substance made of glass fibres and glass flakes widely used in telecommunication, medicine and industry. It is used to insulate glass wool.

Fibre optics

It is a branch of Physics which deals with the transmission of light along the fibres of glass by total internal reflection. Now fibre optics is widely used in telecommunication and medical.

Fibrositis

The term refers to the inflammation of fibrous tissues characterised by pain and stiffness. Anti-inflammatory drugs and aspirin help to relieve the pain.

Fibrous root

It is a type of root which is very small like fibre. It is found in monocot plants, e.g. coconut, grass, bamboo, etc. Unlike dicots there is no main or tap root.

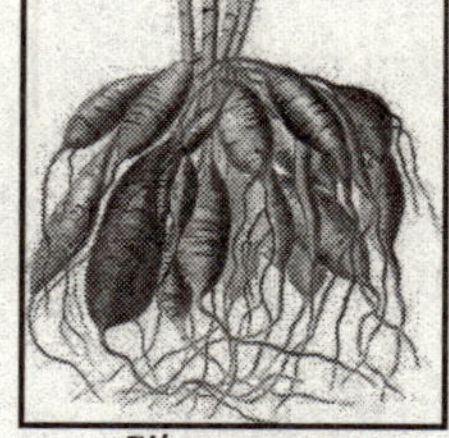

Fibrous root

Filament

It is a wire of high resistance, which when heated to incandescent, acts as a source of light. It is made of tungsten or carbon. It is used in light bulbs and thermionic valves.

File

The term is used for a collection of data stored in a computer. Data can be program files, textual, graphical and numerical.

Filter

It refers to the following:

1. In Chemistry, an apparatus used for separating material from a liquid or gas, e.g. funnel. A porous material like filter paper is also an example of filter.
2. In Physics, it is a device placed in the path of light or other radiation to change frequency distribution.

Filtration

It refers to a process used for separating suspended impurities from a fluid with the help of filter paper, filter funnels, filter flasks, etc.

Fine chemicals

The term is used for the chemicals produced industrially with a high purity. Dyes, drugs are examples of fine chemicals.

Fineness of gold

It is used as a measure of the purity of gold alloy. Usually, it is expressed as parts per thousand. Gold with a fineness of 800% contains 80% gold.

Fire clay

It refers to clay which has small percentage of oxides of calcium, magnesium, iron. It is used in refractory for lining high temperature furnaces.

Fire extinguisher

It is an appliance used for extinguishing fire. It ejects carbon dioxide, water and foam which extinguish fire. Fire extinguishers are of different types, the most commonly used one is the soda-acid type.

Fire extinguisher

Fission

It refers to the following:

1. In physics, it can be defined as a split of a heavy nucleus into lighter nuclei with slight loss of mass, releasing energy which is equivalent to the difference between the rest mass of the neutrons and the fission products and that of the original nucleus. The process of nuclear fission is used in nuclear reactors and atom bombs.
2. 1n biology, it is a type of asexual reproduction occurring in organisms, e.g. diatoms, protozoan and bacteria.

Fixation of nitrogen

It refers to a process in the nitrogen cycle in which atmospheric nitrogen is converted into organic compounds by certain bacteria, particularly in some leguminous plants.

Fixed point

It denotes a temperature that can be precisely reproduced to be used as the basis of a temperature scale. The upper fixed point is 100°C and the lower point is the freezing point 0°C in the Celsius scale.

Fixed star

The term is used for the heavenly bodies which do not appear to change their position on the celestial sphere.

Fizeau, Armand Hippolyte Louis (1819-96)

He was a French Physicist who, in 1845, with Leon Foucault took the first photographs of the sun. In 1849, he measured the speed of light.

Fizeau, Armand Hippolyte Louis

Flame test

It is a simple test used to ascertain the presence of an element by the colour produced in the Bunsen burner flame, for example lithium gives crimson, calcium gives brick red, strontium gives red, etc.

Flammable

The term refers to substances which can catch fire easily, hence they need to be handled carefully, e.g. petroleum.

Flash memory

It is a form of storage in which the device does not need refreshing to maintain the data, but the data is stored even when the power is removed. Flash memory is widely used in digital cameras, storage devices, e.g. USB drives, etc.

Flash point

It is the lowest temperature at which a liquid releases sufficient vapour that can be ignited by an energy source. At flash point a naked flame gives a momentary flash not sustained combustion.

Flatulence

The term is used for the gas formation in the stomach or intestines which causes uneasiness. Antacids are used to help relieve the condition.

Fleming, Sir Alexander (1881-1955)

He was a British Bacteriologist who is widely known for his discovery of antibiotic penicillin in 1928. He studied Medicine at St Mary's Hospital, London and later taught there for the whole of his life. In 1922, he identified lysozyme and enzyme. He was awarded the Nobel Prize for Medicine with Florey and Chain.

Fleming, Sir Alexander

Flight

It can be defined as any form of locomotion in the air – active or passive. Mechanisms of flight are well developed in birds, bats and insects.

Flocculation

It refers to a process in which a particles in colloid join together to form a larger clumps. Flocculating agents, e.g. aluminium sulphate and iron sulphate are used for water purification.

Floppy disc

It is a flexible storage device which has magnetic coat enclosed in a stiff plastic envelop. Data are stored in the magnetic medium on both sides. It is used in a small computer system.

Flower

It is a structure in angiosperms which serves as the reproductive organ. Flowers are highly variable in form, shape, size and colour. Flowers consist of a receptacle which includes petals, stamens, sepals and carpels, etc. Flowers may be monosexual or bisexual.

Labelled fig of flower

Fluid mechanics

The term is used for the study of fluids at rest and in motion. Fluid mechanics is an important science which is used for the study of weather, flight of birds, the swimming of fish apart from aeronautical, chemical, mechanical and civil engineering.

Fluorescein

It is a yellowish red dye with green fluorescence which is used for tracing water flow in water systems and as absorption indicator.

Fluorescent lamp

It is a lamp which produces light by fluorescence. It has a glass tube inside having a coat of fluorescent material. The lamp emits ultraviolet radiation when current flows which further is converted into visible light by the fluorescent material inside.

Fluorescent lamp

Fluoridation

It refers to the process by which a small amount of salts is added to drinking water for preventing dental decay.

Fluorine

It is a non-metallic gas of the halogen group, the atomic number of which is 9; atomic weight 18.9; freezing point - 219.62°C; and boiling point −188.13°C. It is yellow in colour and very toxic and corrosive in nature. Chemically, it is the most electronegative of all elements.

Fluorite

It is a mineral form of calcium fluoride, chiefly used as a flux in smelting of iron and steel and in glass industry. It is also used as a source of fluorine and hydrofluoric acid.

Fluorite

Fluorocarbons

It belongs to a group of synthetic organic compounds obtained by replacing the hydrogen atoms by fluorine atoms. Chemically being resistant, they are suitable to be used as refrigerants, solvents, etc.

Fluxmeter

It is an instrument used for measuring magnetic flux used in conjunction with a coil. It resembles a moving coil galvanometer. Now, it has largely been replaced by one using the Hall probe.

Flyash

The term is used for the non-combustible particles in a gas stream produced as a result of burning of coal or oil. It consists of silica, unburnt carbons, alumina, etc. It is widely used in cement industry. It is a major source of air pollution.

Flyby

It refers to a close approach made by a spacecraft to a satellite or planet without landing or entering the orbit. It is largely done to take photographs or collecting data.

Foam

It can be defined as a substance which produces a very soft mass of small bubbles in a liquid. Some foams are solid, for example rubber.

Focal length (*Symbol* f)

It is the distance between the optical centre or pole of a spherical mirror and its principal focus.

Focus

It refers to the point in an optical system to which light rays converge. Light rays appear to diverge when they pass through a lens or reflected from a mirror.

Fold

It refers to a wave-like form in sedimentary rock which is caused as a result of deformational processes in earth's crust. Fold appears where the rock strata are under horizontal pressures.

Fold

Folic acid

It is a vitamin of vitamin B complex group which is abundantly found in green leafy vegetables, milk, yeast, liver, etc. Its deficiency causes anaemia and normal growth is affected. It is synthesised buy intestinal bacteria.

Follicle

It denote the following:

1. In botany, it refers to a dry dehiscent fruit which splits along one side to release its seed when it is ripe.
2. In anatomy, a cluster of cells which protects and nourishes a cell within. For example hair follicles protecting the roots of the hairs.

Food additive

It is a substance which is added to food to improve its colour, flavour, etc. It is a non-toxic element.

Food chain

It can be defined as a sequence of organisms in an ecosystem in which one eats the one preceding it and is eaten up by the one following it. Thus, producers or the green plants are at the top of the food chain while big carnivores like lion and finally the decomposers make the bottom of the food chain. The position of an organism in a food chain is called its trophic level.

Food preservation

It means prevention of spoilage of food with the help of various techniques such as dehydration, treatment of food with salt, blanching, freezing, freeze drying, irradiation, etc. All these are done to prevent bacterial and fungal decay and contamination of food.

Food reserves

It can be defined as the storage of essential compounds, e.g. fat, protein, carbohydrate for future use. This serves as an important source of energy when required by an organism.

Food web

It is an interconnected system of food chains in which many animals feed at several different trophic levels thus making a complex set of feeding relationship. Usually, a food web does not include decomposers but they are important in the flow of energy in an ecosystem.

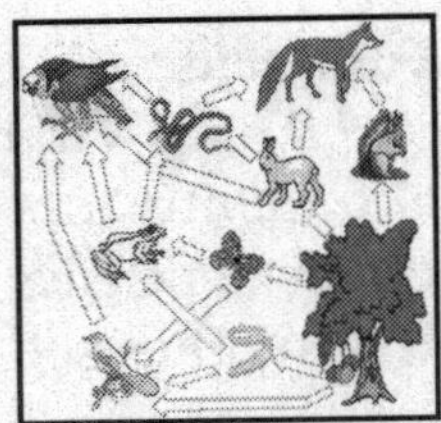

Food web

Foot and mouth disease

It is a serious disease in cattle which is caused by viral infection. Symptoms include eruption in skin, foot and mouth. Vaccination is the effective treatment for the foot and mouth disease.

Force

It refers to any external factor that can change the state of rest or motion of a body. The SI unit of force is the newton.

Forensic science

It is a branch of Science which deals with solving the criminal cases with the help of finger printing, blood analysis, chemical analysis, genetic finger printing, etc.

Forest

Forest

It refers to a large area of vegetation thickly covered with trees of different kinds depending on the temperature and climate of the land. For example, temperate forests may be dominated by deciduous trees, such oak, maple, beech, elm, etc. Forests constitute a major part of biomaess and have significant role in global warming. Forests are a good source of natural resources.

Forging

The term is used for the conversion of hot material into desired shapes and sizes. This is done with the help of compressive force and hydraulic press.

Formaldehyde (*Symbol* CH_2O)

It is a gas with strong smell but is a liquid at $-21°C$. It is used as preservative and in making plastics, dyes and medicine. It is also used as a disinfectant.

Formalin

It is an aqueous solution of formaldehyde used as a preservative for biological specimens and disinfectant.

Formula

It inplies the following:

1. In chemistry, it refers to a way of presenting the chemical composition of a compound using symbols for the atoms an element, e.g. Chlorine: Cl_2. Subscripts represent the numbers of atoms. There are many kinds of formulas, for example, molecular formula, structural formula and empirical formula.
2. In mathematics, it is a rule or law expressed in algebraic symbols.

Fossil

The term is used for the remains of past life including

plants and animals on the earth, but now they are preserved in rocks or ice either by refrigeration or carbonisation. Under the effect of carbonisation or refrigeration the remains form cast like dinosaurs or human imprints in clay or mud, or mineralisation of bones and teeth or shells. Study of fossils is very important as a tool of evolution.

Fossil fuel

It refers to non-renewable sources of energy such as coal, oil and natural gases, formed by the fossilised remains of organisms. Fossil fuels are a major source of greenhouse effect, acid rain and global warming.

Fossil fuel

Foucault's pendulum

It is a simple pendulum in which a heavy metal ball is attached to a long wire and swings freely in any direction to demonstrate the earth's rotation.

f.p.s. units

It is the old system of units in Britain based on foot, pound and second, but now replaced by the SI units for all purposes.

Fraction

It us used for the following:

1. In Mathematics, it is the one or more equal parts of a whole number like 1/12, 1/8 or 1/4, etc.
2. In Chemistry, it refers to the group of similar compounds, which has a common range of boiling points.

Fractionating tower

It is a large tower used in refining crude oil. It makes use of the varying boiling points of the components.

Francium (*Symbol* Fr)

It is a radioactive metallic element belonging to group 1

of the periodic table. Its atomic number is 87; boiling point is 677°C; and melting point: 27°C. It occurs in uranium and thorium ores. It was discovered by Marguerite Perey in 1939.

Franklin, Benjamin (1706-90)

He was an American Scientist who invented the lightning conductor and proved the electrical nature of lightning. Franklin was also a statesman who held various government posts and introduced the concepts of 'positive' and 'negative' with electricity.

Franklin, Benjamin

Freeze-drying

It refers to a process of drying certain substances which are sensitive to heat, e.g. food or plasma. The substance is first deep frozen and then trapped ice is removed by volatilisation under reduced pressure and temperature to avoid any damage.

Freezing mixture

It is a mixture of components which produces a low temperature as result of dissolved salts, e.g. a mixture of ice and sodium chloride. The freezing mixture in contact with ice lowers the melting point of ice.

Freezing point

It refers to the temperature at which a substance is changed from a liquid state to a solid state. For a pure substance, the freezing point and the melting point is the same.

Frequency (*Symbol* f or v)

It can be defined as the rate of repetition of cycles, oscillations or vibrations in a unit time, usually per second which is expressed in hertz. The unit of frequency is hertz.

Frequency modulation

It refers to a process by which the frequency of the carrier is increased or decreased to adjust the signal amplitude which keeps on changing but the carrier amplitude remains constant.

Friction

It refers to the resisting force that opposes the relative motion of two bodies in contact.

Fructose

It is a sweet crystalline substance, occurring in green plants, fruits and honey. It is being widely used as a substitute to sucrose and also in food manufacturing.

Fruit

It is a structure formed from the ovary of a flower, consisting of fruit wall, receptacle, etc. Fruits are divided into two main group – succulent fruits and dry fruits. Succulent fruits are generally dispersed by animals while dry fruits are dispersed by natural agents like wind, water, etc.

Fruit

Fuel

It is used for a substance which can produce a large amount of energy on being oxidised or otherwise changed. Fuels can be solid like wood, coal, or liquid, e.g. petroleum gas, or gas, for example natural gas.

Fuel cell

It refers to a cell which can convert the chemical energy of a fuel directly into electrical energy.

Fumigation

It refers to a process in which bacteria, insects and pests are destroyed by exposing them to toxic chemicals in gaseous state. It is done to food materials to preserve them for long.

Fungi

It is a group of organism, closely related to animals than plants, existing primarily in damp situations. They can be unicellular or multicellular. They lack chlorophyll; hence they are either parasites or saprotrophs on other organisms.

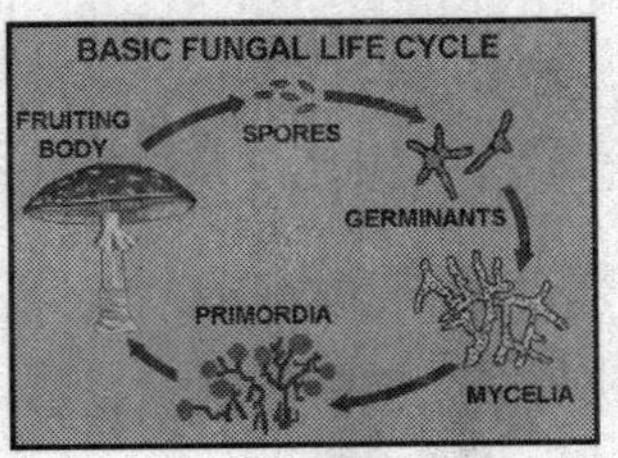

Fungi

Fungicide

It is a chemical used to destroy or prevent the spread of fungal disease in plants and animals.

Fuse

It is a thin wire made of tinned copper or alloy of low melting point used as a safety step to cut the supply of electricity to avoid fire and damage. It is designed to melt at a specified current loading to protect the device or circuit from loading.

Fusel oil

It is a mixture of alcohols, formed as a toxic impurity in the process of alcoholic fermentation. It is used in the manufacturing of plastics, varnishes and paints.

Fusion

It is defined differently in different context:

1. In Physics, it means a change of state of a substance from solid to liquid at specific temperature.
2. In Nuclear physics, the joining together of two atomic nuclei to produce a single heavier nucleus. Thermonuclear weapons like hydrogen bomb work on this principle.

❑

Gabbro

It is a variety of igneous rock which is coarse-grained, and has very similar composition to basalt.

Gabor, Dennis (1900-79)

He was a Hungarian-born British Physicist, who worked on electron microscopes, and invented holography, for which he was awarded the Nobel Prize in 1971.

Gabor, Dennis

Gadolinium (*Symbol* Gd)

It is a silvery-white metallic element in the lanthanide series, with atomic number 64; atomic weight 157.25; melting point 1313°C; and boiling point 3266°C. It occurs in nuclear fission products, and is used in electronic components.

Galactosaemia

It refers to an inborn disorder in human which is known for the tendency to utilise the sugar galactose, resulting in accumulation in blood.

Galactose

It is white crystalline simple sugar occurring in plant polysaccharides, as a product of enzymic digestion of milk sugar.

Galaxy

It is a system of stars formed by association of millions of stars, together with dust and gas held together by gravitational attraction. There are different types of galaxies, namely spiral, elliptical or irregular galaxies. Some galaxies like spiral galaxy have shape but elliptical or irregular galaxies do not have any definite shape. The sun belongs to spiral galaxy.

Galaxy

Galena (*Symbol* pbs)

It is the chief ore of lead, usually occurring as grey metallic cubes mostly in association with copper, zinc, silver, etc.

Galilean telescope

Designed by Italian Astronomer and Physicist Galileo, it was a refracting telescope which has a convex lens as objective and a concave lens as eye-piece. It is no longer used in astronomy.

Gall bladder

It is a muscular pouch attached to the bile duct, storing bile produced from the liver and releasing when food enters the duodenum. It is present in most of the vertebrates.

Gallon

It is a unit for measuring liquid which is equal to about 4.5 litres in the UK and Canada while it is about 3.8 litres in the US.

Gallstone

It refers to small pebble-like structure formed in the gall bladder which blocks the bile duct. It causes intense vomiting and can be cured surgically.

Galvanised iron

The term is used for zinc-coated iron or steel, done mainly for protection from corrosion. Usually, it is carried out by dipping iron plates in molten zinc or by electrolytic process.

Galvanised iron

Galvanometer

It is an instrument used for detecting and measuring small electric currents by deflecting magnetic coils.

Gamma radiation

It refers to electromagnetic radiation of short wavelength, ranging in energy from about 10^{-15} to 10^{-10} emitted by certain radioactive atoms. Gamma radiation has deep penetrating power. Cobalt-60 is a common source of gamma radiation which is used in the treatment of cancer.

Ganglion

The term is used for a mass of nerve tissues like a small ball containing many cell bodies and synapses enclosed in a sheath of connective tissue, occurring in both vertebrates and invertebrates.

Gangrene

The term refers to the death of body tissue because of the supply of oxygen usually caused by an obstruction in blood supply.

Ganja

It is a local name for a powerful illegal narcotic drug obtained from the plant *Cannabis sativa*.

Garnet

It refers to a group of silicate minerals, usually containing calcium, magnesium, manganese, iron, aluminium, chromium, titanium, etc. Some varieties of garnet used as gems and abrasive.

Gas

It refers to a state of matter in which it can move freely and does not have a definite shape either. for example water vapour.

Gas engine

It is used for internal combustion engine which runs on coal, gas, natural gas or producer gas.

Gas laws

The term relates to temperature, pressure as: and volume of an ideal gas. The general gas law is expressed:

Pressure × Volume/Temperature; as: PV/T = K

Gas mask

It is a protective cover usually worn by mine workers over their mouth and nose against the poisonous gases there. The mask has activated carbon gas which absorbs the foul gases.

Gas oil

It refers to petroleum fraction between kerosene and lubricating oil, usually used as domestic and industrial heating fuel. Its density is high and its molecules have up to 25 carbon atoms.

Gas thermometer

It is a device used for measuring gas temperature. It gives the most accurate temperatures in the ranges between 2.5 to 1337 K.

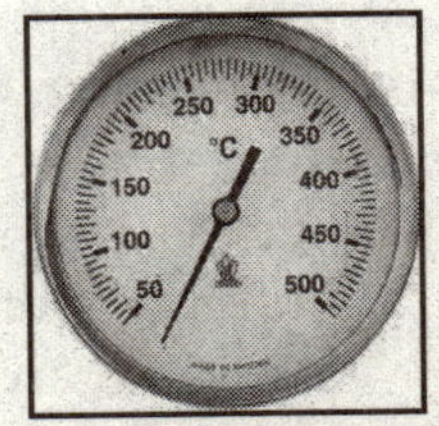

Gas thermometer

Gastrectomy

The term is used for the surgical removal of a part or the whole of stomach, largely because of peptic ulcer.

Gastric juice

It refers to a mixture of inorganic salts, hydrochloric acids and mucus, secreted by the gastric glands in the stomach. It is acidic in nature.

Gastrin

It is a hormone produced in the stomach which has a significant role in the digestive process. It controls the release of gastric juice.

Gastroenteritis

It is an illness of the mucus membrane of stomach and passages, caused by inflammation of the organs. It is characterised by diarrhoea and vomiting.

Gastroenterology

The term relates to the study of the gastrointestinal disorders, including pancreas and liver.

Gastropoda

The term is used for a class of molluscs which includes snails, limpets and land and sea slugs. They have well-developed head and their foot is attached to stomach for locomotion.

Gas turbine

It is an internal combustion engine in which fuel burnt in compressed air supplies hot gas to turn a turbine. It is used in aviation.

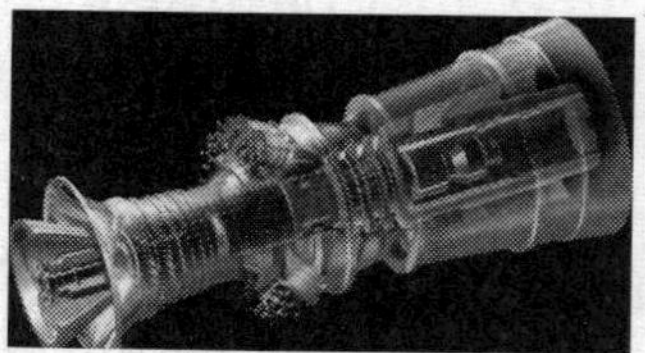

Gas turbine

Gauge

It has different meaning in different context:

1. It is an instrument used for scientific measurement, e.g. wire gauge, pressure gauge.
2. It denotes the width of the railway track, e.g. broad gauge, meter gauge, etc.

Gel

It is a jelly-like coagulated lyophilic colloid, in which the disperse medium has formed a loosely held network of molecules.

Gelatine

It is a water soluble protein produced by hydrolysis of collagen by boiling with water. It is used in photography, pharmacy and in bacteriology for preparing culture media.

Gem

It is a mineral gemstone largely used for decorative purpose. It occurs naturally and is produced artificially as well. Diamond, ruby and sapphire are the examples of gemstones.

Gene

It is a unit of heredity, consisting of DNA, inside a cell. A gene forms a part of chromosome which is the carrier of hereditary features. Genes are changed by mutation. Genes always occur in pairs. If two genes are identical they are called homozygous if not, they are called heterozygous.

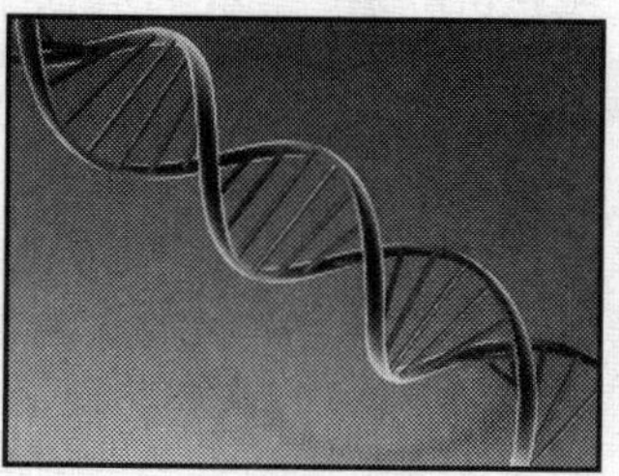

Gene

Gene bank

It refers to a collection of genetic materials, e.g. sperm, frozen embryo, ova, etc. for future use in different fields of study, namely genetic engineering, plant breeding, medicine, etc. The materials are stored in deep freezer.

Gene cloning

It means the production of exact copies of a gene or genes with the help of genetic engineering. Gene cloning facilitates DNA sequencing and is of great help in producing large quantities of desired protein product. For example, the production of human insulin, which is now produced by bacteria containing cloned insulin gene.

Gene mutation

It refers to a change in the nature of a gene happening spontaneously, or it is induced. X-rays, gamma rays and some chemicals induce mutation. A gene in which such a change has occurred is known as a mutant gene or allele.

Gene pool

The term implies all the genes present in a population of a given plant or animal.

Gene therapy

The term refers to the replacement of defective gene with a normal gene with the help of genetic engineering. For gene therapy, a foreign or exogenous DNA is directly introduced into the defective cells or it is done by gene manipulation in which exogenous DNA is delivered into the cell by viruses.

Generator

It is a machine which converts mechanical energy into electrical engineering.

Generator

Genetic code

It refers to the means that transfers the inherited features of parents to offspring. Chromosomes consist of DNA which contains the code bearing cell. There are four different nitrogenous bases present in DNA and messenger RNA, namely thymine, guanine, cytosine and adenine. Some amino acids are the coded by the sequence of three of these bases.

Genetic diseases

It refers to the disorder caused by a fault in the genetic material in the cell. These are transmitted from parents to children. Down's syndrome, Turner's syndrome, haemophilia, etc. are examples of genetic diseases.

Genetic engineering

It refers to the process by which characters of an organism is altered by introducing new genes from another organism into its DNA. It is micromanipulation of genes to get desired change. Genetic engineering has wider application in production of hormones and vaccines, etc. for example commercial insulin. Besides, it is being widely used in agriculture to bring about desired changes in a particular yield.

Genetics

It is the branch of biology which studies heredity and variation in an organism.

Genome project

The term is used to refer the task or project that attempts to get a detailed map and sequence of the entire genetic material in an organism. The bacterium *Haemophilus influenza* was the first organism which was sequenced. Human Genome Project, a multibillion international project, succeeded in producing the sequence of human genome in 2003. This project will bring about a great change in the field of genetic engineering.

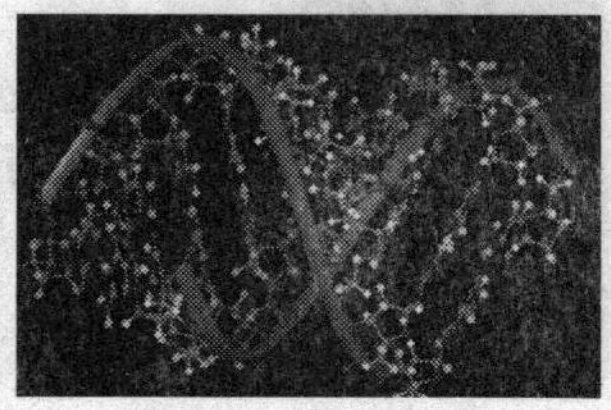

Genome project

Genomics

It is the branch of genetics which deals with the study of genomes.

Genotype

It refers to the inherited genetic composition of an organism which includes the particular combination of alleles or variants that an organism possesses.

Geocentric

It refers to any study in which the earth is regarded at the centre of the universe.

Geochemistry

It deals with the scientific study of the chemical composition of the earth including the earth's elements and their distribution.

Geodynamics

It refers to the study of the motions of the earth, including those of its rotation and crust, mantle and core.

Geography

It refers to the scientific study of the earth's surface and its interaction with man, including the earth's physical and economic features.

Geology

It refers to the study of the history of the earth, its origin, structure and composition, including its rocks, minerals and soils.

Geomagnetism

The term refers to the scientific study of the earth's magnetic field.

Geometry

It is the branch of Mathematics which deals with the properties of space, plane figures and solid figures, including the relationships of lines, angles and surfaces.

Geometry

Geophysics

It is the branch of Science which applies the principles of Physics and Mathematics to the study of the earth. It includes the earth's gravitational field, magnetic field, its interior, winds, tides, volcanoes, earthquakes and their effects on life on earth.

Geostationary orbit

It refers to an orbit of the earth made by an artificial satellite at an altitude of 35900 km, in approximately 24 hours, the period of time equal to earth's period of rotation on its axis. It is used for communication satellites.

Geothermal energy

It refers to the energy generated by heat within the earth's interior, e.g. hot springs, volcanoes, geysers, etc. It is an important source of energy in volcanically sensitive regions like New Zealand, Iceland, etc.

Geothermal energy

Geriatrics

It is the branch of medicine which deals with old age and the related diseases, including the nursing of the old age patients.

Germanium (*Symbol* Ge)

It is a lustrous hard metallic element obtained as a by-product of zinc smelting. Its atomic number is 32; atomic Weight 72.6; melting point 937°C and boiling point 2830°C. It is used as a semiconductor and also in some specialised alloys.

German silver

It is an alloy of copper, zinc and nickel in proportion of 50:25:25. It is used for making cheap jewellery and cutlery.

Germination

It refers to the following:

1. It marks the very early stage in the life of spores and pollen grains when they start to grow.
2. It is the initial stage of the development of a seed to form a seedling under rigid condition of light, moisture and temperature.

Gerontology

It relates to the scientific study of ageing.

Gestation

It refers to the period in mammals from the fertilization of egg to the birth of a young one. The gestation of different animals is different, e.g. in elephant it is 18-22 months, 60 days in cats and about nine months in human beings.

Geyser

It denotes a geothermal feature of the earth which is marked by an opening in the surface of the earth through which there is an intermittent eruption of shower of hot water and steam. Steam is formed in the geyser tube underground when groundwater comes into contact with magma. Increased underground pressure leads to eruption of steam and hot water.

Geyser

Giant planets

The planets of the solar system, namely Saturn, Jupiter, Uranus and Neptune are called giant planets.

Gigantism

It refers to a condition in which a person has unusually abnormal growth leading to a giant formation because of excess of growth hormone.

Gill

It refers to the respiratory organ in the aquatic animals through which they absorb oxygen from the water.

Gingivitis

It is a condition in which the gums become red, swollen and painful, usually caused by dental disease and calculus. It is an early sign of periodontal disease.

Gland

The term is used for a cell or group of cells which is specialised to secret a specific substance vital to the life and function of an organism.

Glass

It refers to a non-crystalline solid – transparent or translucent – made by fusion of silica and other chemicals like barium, borates, potassium, lead or some basic oxides and then cooled suddenly. Glasses are regarded as supercooled liquid.

Glass wool

The term is used for fine glass threads like cotton wool which is both strong and corrosion resistant. It is used for filtering and absorbing corrosive liquid.

Glaucoma

It is an eye disease which causes a gradual loss of eyesight because of the increased pressure of the fluid within the eye ball. It may lead to blindness.

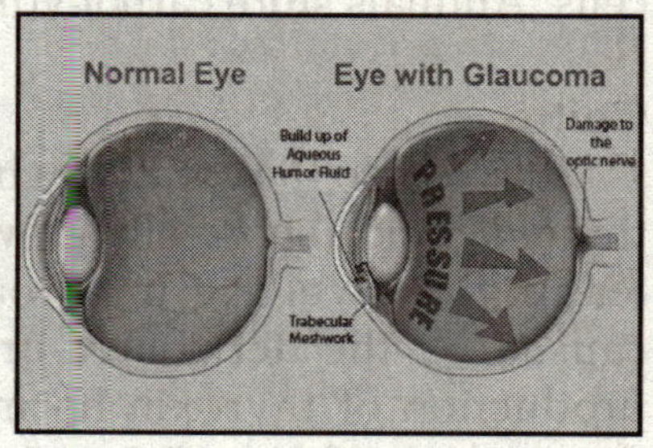

Glaucoma

Global warming

The term denotes an increase in the average air temperature of the earth, largely caused by increased emission of greenhouse gases, e.g. carbon dioxide, chlorofluorocarbons (CFC), and harmful gases. It has serious implications, e.g. changes in global climate pattern, melting of ice masses with consequent rising in sea levels. Average global surface temperature increased over the 20th by about 0.6°C and is predicted to rise between 1.4°C and 5.8°C during a period of one century.

Glottis

In vertebrates, it is the opening from the pharynx to trachea which also serves as a space for vocal cords in mammals.

Glucagon

It refers to the polypeptide hormone secreted by the islets of Langerhans in the pancreas. It stimulates the breakdown of glycogen in the liver and maintains blood sugar. It influences the effect of insulin.

Glucose

It is a naturally occurring white crystalline sugar, present in plants and animals. It is a major source of energy for a living organism. It is a carbohydrate with chemical formula $C_6H_{12}O_6$. In plants, it is produced during photosynthesis and stored as starch.

Glycogen

It is a soluble polysaccharide occurring in liver and muscle cells. Animals store carbohydrate as glycogen.

Goitre

It refers to the condition in which thyroid gland abnormally grow in size leading to swelling in throat. It is caused by the deficiency or excess production of thyroxin hormone by due to lack of insufficient intake of iodine. Symptoms include weight gain or loss, nervousness, tiredness, palpitation, etc.

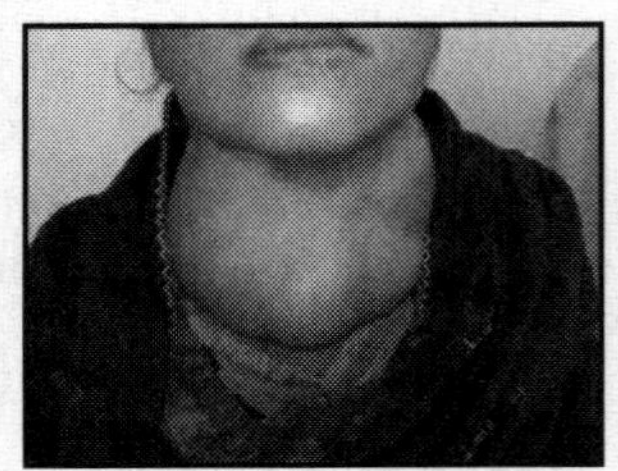

Goitre

Gold

Gold

It is a soft yellow malleable metallic element, the atomic number of which is 79; atomic weight 197.0; melting point 1064.43°C and boiling point 2807±2°C. This precious metal is ductile, non-corrosive and dissolves in aqua regia. It occurs as free metal in mines and also present in lead and copper sulphide ores. It is widely used in jewellery, dentistry and electronic devices.

Gonorrhoea

It is venereal disease caused by sexual contact with an infected person. Women are more affected than men. Symptoms include painful urination, pain in genital organ, etc. Penicillin is used as an effective drug for the treatment of this disease.

Gout

It is a disease which causes painful swelling in the joints especially knees, toes, fingers, etc. caused by the deposition of uric acid and urates which are deposited there as a result of metabolic disorder.

Governor

It is a device which controls the speed of a motor or an engine despite variation in load. It works on the principle of negative feedback.

Graft

It denotes the transplantation of living tissue in the same or the different organism. Grafting of plant tissue is a common horticulture practice, largely done for propagation of the plant. In animals and humans, graft is used to replace the damaged part or organ of the body.

Graham's law

The law states that the rates of diffusion of a gas are inversely proportional to the square roots of its densities. This principle is used in separating isotopes. The law is named after the Scientist Thomas Graham who formulated in 1829.

Gram

It is a unit of mass equal to one thousandth of a kilogram. In c.g.s. units gram is the fundamental unit of mass.

Granite

It is a variety of igneous rock containing mica, quartz and feldspar. It is extremely hard light coloured ranging from grey, white to pink, generally resulting from slow solidification of molten magma. It is widely used in building construction.

Graphite

It is a soft mineral black in colour with melting point 3650°C, which is a good conductor of heat and electricity. It is a natural isotope of carbon used in making electrodes and as a moderator in reactor.

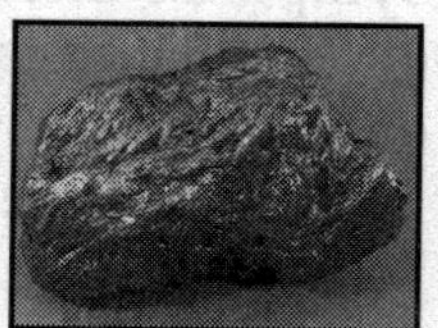

Graphite

Gravitation

It is defined as a force of mutual attraction between two bodies in universe. It depends on their masses and the distance between them.

Gray (*Symbol* Gy)

It is the derived SI unit of ionising radiation which is equal to the energy in joules absorbed by one kilogram of irradiated material. It is named after the British Scientist L.H. Gray.

Greenhouse effect

It refers to the effect occurring in the atmosphere because of the presence of certain gases, namely carbon dioxide, nitrogen oxides, methane, chlorofluorocarbons and ozone, emitted from factories and vehicles. The presence of these gases traps the infrared radiation coming out from the sun causing an increase in the temperature of the atmosphere thus leading to global warming. Greenhouse effect is a grave environmental concern. The increase in temperature has a far-reaching impact on global weather pattern and agricultural yield.

Grid

It denotes the following:

1. It refers to the system of overhead wires or cables used for transmission and distribution of electrical power.
2. In cartography, it is used for a network of horizontal and vertical lines on a map that denotes a specific point.

Growth hormone

It is the hormone secreted by the pituitary gland which stimulates the growth of long bones, promotes the use of fats and helps in protein synthesis. Excess production of growth hormone results in gigantism while its deficiency causes dwarfism.

Gum

It refers to a substance obtained from plants which forms sticky solution with water. Gums are mostly complex polysaccharides. Gums provide a temporary protective covering.

Gum

Gun metal

It is a type of bronze containing 80-90% copper; 8-10% tin and 2-4% zinc, used to make canons, pipes, bearings, etc. because of its resistance to wear and corrosion.

Gun power

It is an explosive consisting of a mixture of potassium nitrate, sulphur and charcoal. It is no longer used as explosive but it is the basis of fireworks.

Gynaecology

It is the branch of medical science which studies the diseases of women especially the female reproductive organs.

Gypsum

It is the mineral form of hydrated calcium sulphate which is used in cement, paper and rubber industry. It is also used in plaster of Paris and in building construction.

Gyroscope

It is a spinning body which can resist torques altering the alignment of spin axis. It is used for stabilising a ship, aircraft or platform.

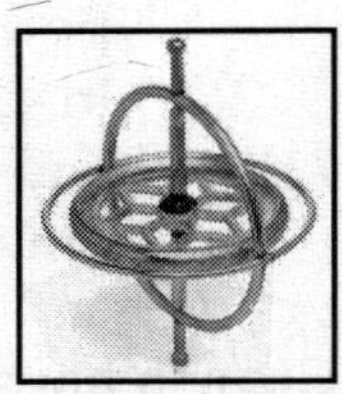

Gyroscope

H

It is a symbol for hydrogen, Henry and magnetic field strength.

Haber, Fritz (1868-1934)

He was a German Chemist who being a jew had to go to exile in Britain in 1933 where he worked in Cambridge. He developed the Haber process for which he was awarded the Nobel Prize for Chemistry in 1938.

Habitat

It refers to the physical environment in which an organism lives and grows. The organism gets all required things of its survival there.

Haem

It is the iron-containing molecule which with proteins form haemoproteins.

Haematite

It is the most important ore of iron usually occurring in two main forms – massive kidney-shaped ore and metallic crystals. Haematite is a colouring agent in rocks. It is used as polishing agent and paint.

Haematite

Haematology

It is the branch of Medicine which studies the formation, composition, function and disease of blood and blood constituents.

Haemoglobin

It is the red substance in the blood which contains iron and carries oxygen throughout the body. Lack of haemoglobin causes anaemia in humans.

Haemophilia

It is a sex-linked disease in which the blood clots very slowly because of the deficiency of Factor VII. The disease largely affects the male children. It is a hereditary disease which is also called Christmas disease.

Hafnium (*Symbol* Hf)

It is a silvery white lustrous metal with atomic number 72; atomic weight 178.49; melting point 2277 ± 20°C; boiling point 4602°C. The metal is found with zirconium and is used in tungsten filament and as a neutron absorber.

Hair follicle

The term is used for tubular depression in skin of mammals which contains the root of a hair. It has its base in subcutaneous tissue but it is lined with epidermal cells.

Hahn, Otto (1879-1968)

He was a German Chemist who discovered protactinium in 1917 with Lise Meitner. He also worked with Fritz Strassmann and worked on uranium bombardment. In 1944, he was awarded the Nobel Prize for Chemistry.

Hahn, Otto

Hair

It is a multicellular thread-like structure produced by the epidermis in skin in mammals. It is composed of dead keratinized cells. Hair reduces heat loss thus helps in maintaining the body temperature.

Half life

It refers to the time that a radioactive substance takes for 50% of its decay or the time a radioactive source takes to decay to half its original value. There is a huge variation in time which may vary from millionth of a second to the billions of years, for example, uranium-238, thorium-232.

Halite

The term is used for the naturally occurring sodium chloride which is colourless but in pure form it is blue.

Halley'comet

It is a bright comet which moves around the sun in the opposite direction to the planets. It is named after Edmund Halley who first calculated its orbit in 1705. It takes about 76 years to orbit the sun. It last appeared in 1986.

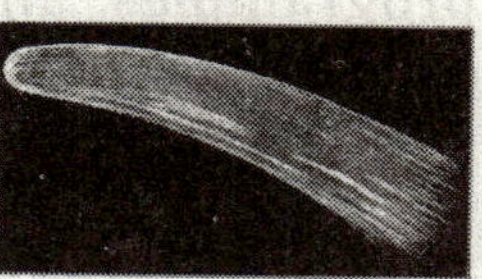

Halley'comet

Hallucinogen

The term refers to drugs that cause alterations in perception usually visual, but in mood and thought as well, e.g. lysergic acid, mescaline, etc.

Halo

The term is used for the ring of bright light often seen around the sun or the moon. It is caused by the diffraction of light by the particles present in the atmosphere.

Halogen

It refers to a group of five elements, namely chlorine, fluorine, iodine, bromine and astatine which react with hydrogen to form acids from which salts can be produced. The elements have similar chemical properties. Halogens as a gas are used in lamps and stoves.

Halophyte

It belongs to a group of plants which can adapt to life in

soils with high concentration of salt, e.g. marshes and mudflats. Examples of halophytes are mangrove trees, rice grass, sea lavender, etc.

Hard copy

The term refers to the output preserved in a permanent form, usually as a printout, rather than preserved temporarily as on disk or display terminal.

Hard disk

It is a device used for storage of programmes and documents in a computer. It is a rigid metal disk with magnet coat on it.

Hard glass

It is a kind of glass which has content of potassium and high silica. It is used in glassware industry.

Hardening of oils

The term is used for the process of converting liquid oils to solid by hydrogenation.

Hardness of water

It denotes the quality of water which indicates high concentration of alkaline salts in water, mainly calcium and magnesium. Hardness of water prevents the formation of lather and causes problems by reducing the efficiency of soap, detergent, etc. There are two types of hardness: (i) temporary hardness, caused by the presence of bicarbonates of metals, which can be removed by boiling the water; and (ii) permanent hardness, which is caused by the sulphates of metals. It can be removed by using washing soda which precipitates the carbonates.

Hardware

The term includes physical, mechanical, elecromechanical and electrical equipment including all permanent components of a computer and data processing system as opposed to software consisting of programmes and data, i.e. intangible component.

Hare's apparatus

It is a type of hydrometer used for measuring the relative densities of two liquids. It was invented by US Chemist Robert Hare.

Harvey, William (1578-1657)

He was an English physician who is best known for discovering the circulation of blood. He worked at the Bartholomew's hospital and also served as a court physician.

Hawking, Stephen William (1942-)

He is a British Cosmologist and Physicist who later became Lucasian Professor of Mathematics at Cambridge. His area of speciality is big bang and black hole. He showed that black holes can emit particles by the Hawking process. He is a well known author of great science works: *A Brief History of Time* and *The Universe in a Nutshell*.

Hawking, Stephen William

Hay fever

It is a form of allergic rhinitis which affects nose, eyes and throat. It is caused by the pollen from the plants which is present in the air and when that air is breathed in. Antihistamines are used to treat the disease.

Heart

It is a hollow muscular organ which is at the centre of the circulatory system in animals. It circulates blood throughout the blood vessels by regular rhythmic contractions. In vertebrates, the heart is composed of specialised muscle. In mammals and birds, the heart has four chambers, two auricles and two ventricles. In fish, the heart is two-chambered while in amphibians and reptiles, the heart has three chambers.

Human heart is complex and is controlled by the autonomous nervous system.

Heart-lung machine

It is a machine used during cardiac surgery to perform the function of heart for some time. Its main function is purification of blood and removal of carbon dioxide.

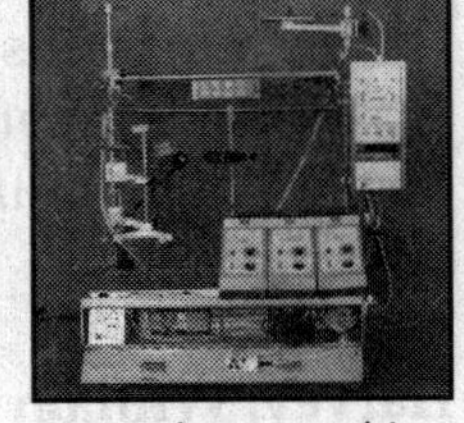

Heart-lung machine

Heat

It refers to the energy that a substance possesses in the form of kinetic energy. Also the process of energy transfer from one body or system to another because of difference in temperature. The units of heat are joules or calories.

Heat engine

It refers to a device which converts heat into energy. The heat is produced by the combustion of a fuel. In an internal combustion engine the fuel is burnt inside the engine while in a steam engine the fuel raises the steam outside the engine and some of the energy is used to do work inside the engine.

Heat transfer

It refers to the process of the transfer of energy from one body to the another by conduction, convection or radiation. The transfer of energy is mainly caused by the difference in temperature.

Heavy metal

The term is used for a metal which has high atomic mass, usually applied to metals such as zinc, lead and copper. These metal cause environmental pollution.

Heavy water

It refers to the water which contains heavier hydrogen isotopes deuterium (D) instead of normal hydrogen isotope H. Its physical properties are different from those of normal water. It is used as a moderator in nuclear reactors.

Helium (*Symbol* He)

It is a colourless odourless gaseous non-metallic element of group 18 of the periodic table atomic no.: 2; atomic weight: 4; melting point: " 272.2°C and boiling point: " 268.93°C. The element has the lowest boiling point of all the substances and it is the second most abundantly found element in the universe. Chemically it is totally inert and is used as refrigerant in superconductors and also in filling balloons.

Helminthology

The term refers to the scientific study of the worms especially the parasitic worms.

Hematite

It is the chief ore of iron, i.e. iron oxide.

Henry (*Symbol* H)

It is the SI unit of mutual inductance. It is named after Joseph Henry.

Henry, Joseph (1797-1878)

He was a US physicist who later became professor of natural philosophy at Princeton. In 1830 he discovered electromagnetic induction and, in 1832 self-induction. He invented an electric motor in which he used insulated windings to produce electromagnet. In 1835, he invented the electric relay.

Henry, Joseph

Heparin

The term is used for a glycosaminoglycan, a complex anticoagulant, present especially in vertebrates' lungs and blood vessels. It is used in the treatment of thrombosis.

Hepatitis

It is a serious disease of the liver with symptoms like fever, gastrointestinal problems, etc. It is caused by virus or chemical present in alcohol. There are mainly three types of hepatitis:

hepatitis A, hepatitis B, and hepatitis C; the last two being the most serious.

Herbicides

The term include substances which are used to inhibit the growth of unwanted herbs or plants.

Herbivore

It refers to an animal that feeds on vegetation. Herbivores have teeth adapted for grinding vegetation and have such alimentary canals which can digest cellulose.

Hereditary disease

The term is used for the diseases which are genetically transmitted from parents to offspring, e.g. colour blindness, diabetes, haemophilia, cystic fibrosis, etc.

Hereditary

It can be defined as the transmission of characteristics from parents to offsprings through genetic material, i.e. chromosomes. The first scientific study of hereditary was undertaken by Gregor John Mendel.

Hermophrodite

The term includes the plants or animals which have both male and female reproductive organ. Earthworm is an example of hermophrodite animal.

Hermophrodite

Heroin

It is a powerful narcotic derived from morphine. It is highly addictive, and is also used as analgesic.

Hertz (*Symbol* Hz)

It is the SI unit of frequency. Named after Heinrich Hertz, it is the number of oscillations per second of a vibrating system.

Heterodont

It refers to animals which have many different types of teeth, e.g. canine teeth, premolars, incisors. Each type has their different function. Mammals are mostly heterodont.

Heterodont

Heterozygote

The term is used for an individual who has two different alleles in the two corresponding loci on chromosomes.

Hexamine

It is a colourless crystalline solid made by the condensation of methanol with ammonia. It is soluble in water and has been used as antiseptic and as a solid fuel for camping stoves. It is used in plastic industry.

Hibernation

It refers to a period of dormancy or sleep-like state in animals to pass terrible cold of winter months, when various physiological changes like lowering of metabolism, pulse rate and other vital processes occur, to survive on the reserve of body fat.

Hiccup

It refers to sharp, usually repeated sound made by involuntary contraction of diaphragm accompanied with sudden closing of glottis.

High frequency

It denotes the radio frequency, which has a wavelength in the range of 10-100 meters. Usually, it is in the range of 3-30 megahertz.

High speed steel

It is a variety of very hard steel, consisting of 12 to 22% tungsten, up to 5% chromium, carbon, vanadium and molybdenum. It remains hard even at red heat, hence used for cutting tools.

Hinge joint

In vertebrates, it is a joint which allows free movement in one plane only, e.g. the elbow joint.

Histamine

The term is used for a substance which is formed from the amino acid histidine. It is present in all tissues but is concentrated in connective tissues and is released during allergic reaction. It causes dilation and permeability of blood vessels resulting in itching, sneezing, localized swelling, running nose, etc. Anti-histamine drugs help to counter the symptoms.

Histology

It refers to the scientific study of the tissues of living organisms – plants and animals.

Hodgkins disease

It is a serious disease of lymphatic tissues characterised by enlargement of lymph nodes affecting liver, spleen, and bone marrow. It can be treated by surgery, chemotherapy and radiotherapy.

Holography

It is a method of producing three-dimensional images of an object using two set of diffracted waves, one forming the virtual image and the other forming a real image on the other side of a plate. The holograms produce three-dimensional images when laser is projected through them. This method was invented by Dennis Gabor in 1948.

Homodont

The term is used for animals who have their teeth all of the same shape, frogs. Most of the vertebrates are homodont, except mammals.

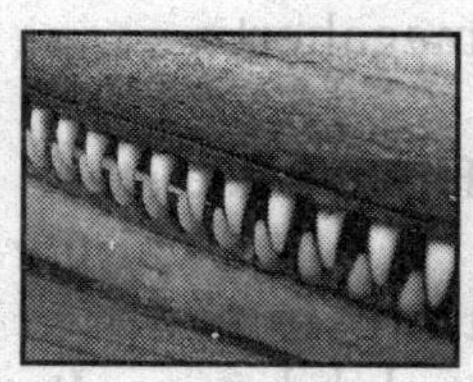

Homodont

Homologous organs

The term denotes the organs which have the similarity in structure and functions, e.g. forelimbs of man, bat, monkey, etc.

Hormone

It is a chemical substance produced in small quantities into the bloodstream by an endocrine gland, for example-insulin is secreted by pancreas. Hormones have significant role in the growth and functioning of specific cells and tissues. The deficiency or the excess of any hormones affect the normal functioning in human.

Horsepower

It is an Imperial unit of power, now replaced by watt. It is equal to 745.7 watts.

Horticulture

It refers to the scientific study of growing flowers, fruit and vegetables.

Host

The term is used for an organism whose body serves as a source of food and shelter for a parasite. There are two types of host - definitive, in which a parasite becomes sexually mature; and intermediate, in which a parasite passes the initial stage of its life cycle.

HT line

It is an electric line which carries high tension current.

Hubble space telescope

It is an astronomical telescope launched in April 1990 in joint collaboration of NASA and European Space Agency to provide images and data about the universe in visible, infrared and ultraviolet ranges.

Hubble space telescope

HIV (Human Immunodeficiency Virus)

It is the virus which causes AIDS in human. HIV is said to have originated in Africa.

Humidity

The term is used for the concentration of water vapour in the atmosphere. It is expressed as absolute humidity and relative humidity which is actually the ratio of moisture in air.

Humus

It refers to a complex brown colloidal matter present in soil which adds to its fertility. It is formed by the decomposition of animal, microbial and vegetative substance.

Hurricane

It refers to the tropical cyclone with speed of 117 km/hour which causes heavy damage and destruction.

Hurricane

Hybrid

The term denotes a plant or an animal produced from the mating in which parents differ at least in one feature. Hybrid between different animal species is generally infertile.

Hydration

The term is used for a combination of water and another substance.

Hydraulics

It is the branch of science which studies the properties of water and other fluids, at rest or in motion with particular focus to their application in engineering. The study is based on the principle that pressurised fluid increases the mechanical efficiency.

Hydrocarbons

The term refers to chemical compounds which consist only of hydrogen and carbon, e.g. alkenes, alkanes, alkynes, etc. Hydrocarbons are derived from petroleum and coal tar.

Hydrochloric acid (*Symbol* HCL)

It is a colourless acidic gas which is a solution of HCL in water. It is a monobasic acid which forms only one salt with metals.

Hydrocooling

It is a method of cooling fruits and vegetables in which they are first immersed in ice water and then subjected to vacuum.

Hydrodynamics

The term refers to the mathematical study of the forces, energy and the pressure of fluids in motion and the interaction of such fluids with their boundaries.

Hydroelectric power

The term denotes the electricity produced by using the power of water. To produce hydroelectricity, flowing water is used to turn the turbine in magnetic field. The turbines are coupled to generators.

Hydrogen (*Symbol* H)

It is a colourless, odourless gas which is the lightest and the most abundantly found element in the universe; atomic no: 1; atomic weight: 1; melting point: –259.14° boiling point: "252.87°C. Hydrogen accounts for 935 of the total number of atoms and 93% of the total mass. Hydrogen is used as a fuel in rocket, in wielding and also in hardening of fats and oils. Besides, it is also used in other industrial processes such as the refining of petroleum and the reduction of oxide ores.

Hydrogen bomb

It refers to a bomb based on the principle of nuclear fusion. In hydrogen bomb, hydrogen nuclei are used to form helium nuclei which release thermonuclear energy.

Hydrogen bomb

Hydrological cycle

The term refers to cyclic circulation of water between the atmosphere, land and oceans on the earth via evapotranspiration, precipitation and through run-off into various water bodies such as streams, rivers, lakes and ultimately to the oceans. Water evaporates from the water bodies to condense and form clouds which come back to the earth as rainfall, hail, snow, etc. Some part of it returns to the oceans and some of it flows down the underground and forms groundwater storage.

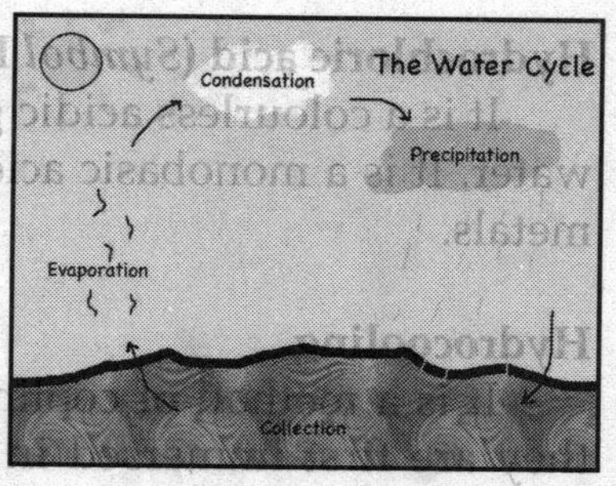

Hydrological cycle

Hydrology

It refers to the scientific study of water, including its occurrence, movement and properties in the hydrosphere and atmosphere.

Hydrometer

It is an instrument used for measuring the density or relative density of liquids. It consists of a glass tube and a weighted bulb at the end which helps it float vertically in a liquid.

Hydrophyte

The term is used for plants which either grows in wet soil or partially or fully submerged in water. Water lilies and pond weeds are the examples of hydrophytes.

Hydroponics

It refers to a technique which is used to grow plants in culture medium rather than soil.

Hydrosphere

The term is used to refer all of the water on the surface of the earth including seas, oceans, rivers, lakes, ice caps and glaciers, etc.

Hydrostatics

The term is used for the scientific study of fluids at rest, including pressure and forces with particular focus to dams, storage tanks, and hydraulic machinery.

Hygrometer

It is an instrument used for measuring the humidity of the atmosphere.

Hygrometer

Hygroscope

It is an instrument which is used to show the variations of relative humidity in the air.

Hyper-

It is a prefix which expresses excess of anything, for example, in the sense of over, above, high, as in hypertension, hyperactive, hypersensitive.

Hypermetropia

The term refers to a defect of vision in which the person is not able to see an object close to him. It is usually caused by the shortness of eyeball when the images are formed behind the retina. Spectacles with converging lens are used to correct the defect which helps to focus the image onto the retina.

Hypothalamus

It is the part of the vertebrate brain located the thalamus and the cerebrum. It regulates body temperature, water balance, sleeping, feeding and neuroendocrine system.

Hypsometer

It is a device used for calibrating thermometers at the boiling point of water. It can also be used to measure altitude. ❑

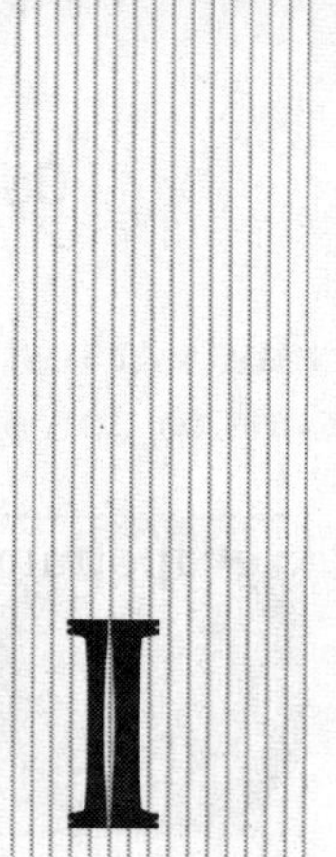

Ice age

It represents a period in earth's history during which ice advanced towards equator leading to a general fall in temperature. At least four major ice ages had occurred during the Pleistocene period, and the last major ice age ended about 10,000 years ago.

Ice point

It is the temperature at which water and ice are in equilibrium at standard atmospheric pressure, i.e. 0°C in the Celsius scale.

Ideal gas

The term is used for a gas which obeys the ideal gas law. It is a hypothetical gas which would have infinitely small molecules with negligible forces between them.

Identical twins

These are the twins which develop from the single fertilized egg. The twins have identical DNA sequences.

Igneous rocks

The term includes the rocks which are formed from volcanic eruption and the crystallization of magma, e.g. granite, basalt, gabbro, etc.

Igneous rocks

Image

It refers to visual appearance of an object formed by a mirror, lens, or any optical system. The image can be real or virtual.

Immunity

The term is used for the acquired or intrinsic mechanism of an animal which helps it to resist an infective agent or its harmful effects. The immunity depends on the defensive cell, i.e. antibodies and lymphocytes which produce an immune response.

Immunoglobulin

It is a protein present in blood and other blood fluid, produced by specialised white blood cells. They act as antibodies and help it from infective agents. There are different kinds of immunoglobulin such as IgA, IgD, IgE, etc.

Imperial units

The term refers to the British system of units based on the pound and the yard. It is also called foot-pound-second system which is now being replaced by metric units.

Implant

It refers to a device, tissue or a substance which is inserted into the body either to replace the existing one or to help it in its normal functioning, for medical purposes usually by operation. Pacemakers, drug implants are the examples of implant.

Inclinometer

It is an instrument used for measuring the angle of inclination that an aircraft makes while flying.

Inclinometer

Incubation

The term is used for the following:

1. The process of maintaining a culture of organisms at

the temperature required for its growth.

2. The process of maintaining the fertilised eggs of some animals at the required temperature for the successful development of embryos.

Index fossil

The term refers to fossils, mainly present in the sedimentary rocks, that existed during a particular span of geological time and is of importance to date the rock in which it is found.

Induction coil

It is a device used for producing high-voltage alternating current from a low-voltage direct current with the help of electromagnetic induction. This is widely used in a spark-ignition internal combustion engine of a car to produce high-voltage producing spark to ignite the fuel.

Induction coil

Inert gases

The term includes rare gases or monatomic gaseous elements of group 18, formerly group 0 of the periodic table. These gases are helium, krypton, neon, argon and xenon. These gases have special electron configuration which makes them chemically inert.

Infection

It refers to the invasion of a disease by microorganisms, e.g. pathogen which establishes and multiply themselves, sometimes even without symptoms. Antibiotics and antiseptics are used for the treatment of infections.

Infertility

It refers to the inability of an organism to produce its young ones, either because of physical or psychological factors.

Influenza

It is an infectious disease which mainly affects the respiratory organs. It is caused by virus which is transmitted by sneezing and coughing. Its symptoms include headache coupled with fever, weakness, loss of appetite and body pain.

Infrared radiation

It is the electromagnetic radiation which has a wavelength longer than the red light in the range of 0.7 micrometer to 1 millimeter. It was discovered by William Herschel in 1800.

Infrasound

The term is used for sound-like waves in the frequency range of about 20 hertz which is below the audible limit.

Inoculation

It means introduction of weak microorganisms into the body so as to produce antibodies to boost up the immunity against certain infectious diseases e.g. small pox.

Insecticide

The term refers to a chemical that destroys insects which are harmful to plants, DDT, aldrin, malathion, etc.

Insulator

It refers to a material or device that is a poor conductor of heat, electricity or sound.

Insulin

It is a protein hormone secreted in the body by the beta cells of islets of Langerhans in the pancreas. It controls the amount of sugar in the blood. Inadequate amount of insulin leads to an increase in the level of sugar in the blood and urine which is called diabetes mellitus.

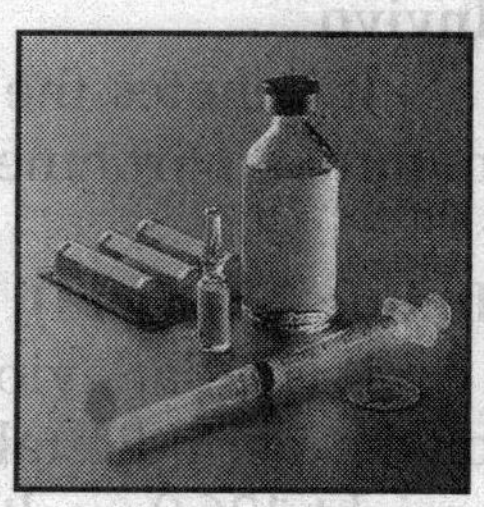

Insulin

Interferometer

It is an instrument which produces optical interference fringes used for measuring wavelengths, small distances and testing flats. The instrument is used for making precision instruments.

Interferometer

Internal combustion engine

It is an engine in which fuel is burnt in the combustion chamber within the engine, rather than in separate chamber, e.g. petrol and diesel engine.

Internet

The term used for a worldwide network of computer connecting other networks and computers from various institutions and organisations. It offers services to servers which primarily interconnect other networks, and not the users.

Invertebrate

The term includes animals which do not have vertebral column, i.e. backbone. About 95% of the animal species come in this category which includes sponges, echinoderms, primitive aquatic chordates, etc.

Invitro

It refers to the biological process which takes place outside a living body usually in a scientific apparatus, e.g. invitro fertilization in which mature egg cells are fertilized externally in case of those woman who are unfit to conceive.

Invivo

It denotes the biological process which takes place in a natural environment, i.e. living body.

Iodine (*Symbol* I)

It is a dark violet metallic element belonging to group 17 of the periodic table, which has atomic number 57; atomic weight 126.9; melting point: 113.5°C; boiling point 184.35°C.

Iodine is required as a trace element in a living organisms. The element is present in sea water and sea weed. It is used as antiseptic and in photographic film.

Ionising radiation

It refers to the ionising radiation which has high penetrating power, e.g. gamma rays, short wave x-rays, etc.

Ionosphere

It refers to a layer of the earth's atmosphere extending between 80 to 100 km above the surface of the earth. Free electrons arrive there from ionisation caused by ultraviolet radiation coming from the sun. This layer reflects the radio wave which enables radio transmission.

Iris

It is the pigmented part of the eye in vertebrates while in optics, it refers to the diaphragm over the lens.

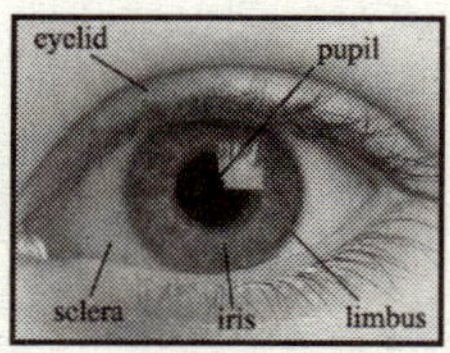

Iris

Irradiation

It means an exposure to a body to radiation, usually ionising radiation.

Irrigation

It means provision of water for agriculture through man-made system of water supply, for example by canals, pipeline system, ditches, etc. Irrigation can increase soil sanity. Usually, the arrangements are required when water needs are not fulfilled by rainfall.

Islets of Langerhans

The term is used for the group of cells in the pancreas which function as an endocrine gland. The alpha cells secrete glucagon, the beta cells secrete insulin and the D cells secrete somatostatin. It is named after its discoverer German Anatomist Paul Langerhans.

Isotones

The refers to the nucleotide which contains the same number of neutrons but different number of protons, e.g. hydrogen, deuterium.

IT (Information Technology)

It refers to the wider use of the study and application of electronic equipment, computers, etc for storing, transmission and analysing data—numerical, textual, visual or audio.

IT (Information Technology)

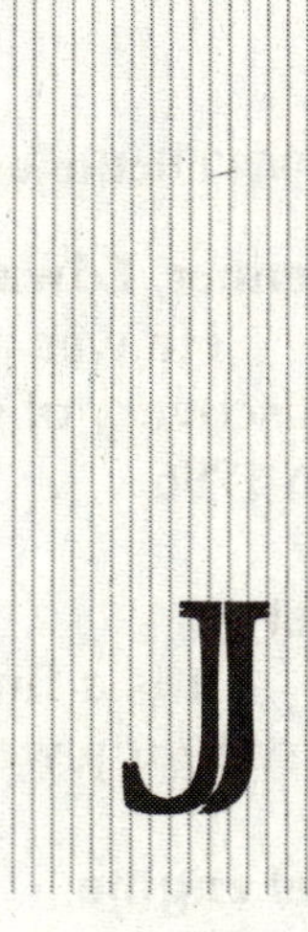

J

It is the symbol for joule and also for magnetic polarisation.

Jade

It is a hard, semiprecious stone usually green in colour used in making jewellery and decorative objects. Jade consists of sodium aluminium silicate and is also found in white, brown and orange colour.

Jade

Jasper

It is a red mineral associated with iron ores, used as a gemstone. It is an impure variety of chalcedony.

Jaundice

It is a liver disease caused when the bile duct is affected either by infection or stone formation resulting in high bilirubin in blood and urine. Symptoms include yellow colour of skin, eyes accompanied with loss of appetite, weakness, etc.

Jejunum

It is the portion of mammalian small intestine which comes next to duodenum and is followed by ileum. It contains numerous outgrowths which absorb digested food.

Jenner, Edward (1749-1823)

He was a British Physician who is widely known for his discovery of smallpox vaccine which he introduced in Britain in 1796.

Jet

It is a fine variety of coal which is cut and polished and used for jewellery.

Jet engine

It refers to an engine which drives an aircraft forward by producing a stream of hot air or gases behind it by reaction propulsion.

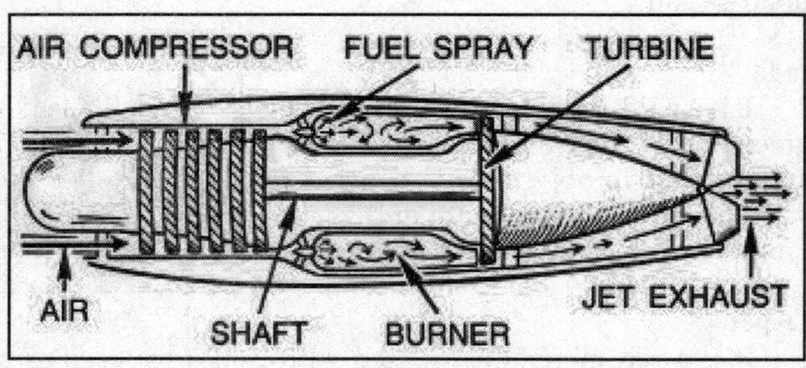

Jet propulsion

It means the moving forward of a body by means of a force which is produced by discharging a fluid in jet form. It works on the Newton's third law of motion which states that every action there is an equal and opposite reaction. Jet propulsion is widely used in aircraft and spacecraft and is the only method of propulsion in space.

Jeweller's rouge

The term refers to red powdered haematite (Fe_2O_3) which is a mild abrasive. It is used in polishes and metal cleaners.

Joint

It is the point where two bones meet with tissues that surround it. There are many types of joint, for example hinge joints, pivot joint, ball and socket joint, etc. Some joints are moveable and some are immoveable.

Joliot-Curie, Irene (1897-1956)

She was a French Physicist and daughter of Marie and Pierre Curie who began her career at the Radium Institute and later rose to become its Director. She married Frederick Joliot in 1926 and was awarded the Nobel Prize for Chemistry with her husband in 1935 for their discovery of the artificial radioactivity.

Joliot-Curie, Irene

Joule (*Symbol* J)

It is the SI unit of work and energy. It is equal to the work done when the point of application of a force of one Newton moves through a distance of one meter in the direction of the force. 1 joule is equal to 10^7 or 0.2388 calorie.

Jupiter

It is the largest planet in the solar system and the fifth in order of distance from the sun. Its equatorial diameter is 1,42,985 km and mass is 1.889×10^{27} kg or 318 times that of the earth. The planet has at least 63 satellites and it rotates anticlockwise once every six earth days.

Jurassic

It refers to the second geological period of the Mesozoic era when the reptiles were dominant on the earth.

❑

K

It is a symbol of potassium; Kelvin; velocity constant; thermal conductivity.

Kala-azar

It is a disease common in tropical countries which is caused by protozoan and transmitted by sandflies. Its symptoms include prolonged fever, anaemia accompanied with enlargement of spleen and liver. Antimony compound is effective in the treatment of kala-azar.

Kaolin

It is soft white clay chiefly composed of the kaolinite mineral widely used in ceramics industry, besides rubber paper, textiles and paint and in medicines as well.

Kaolin

Karyotype

The term is used for the number and structure of the chromosomes in a cell. It is identical in all the diploid cells of an organism.

Katharometer

It is a device used for comparing the thermal conductivities of two gases. It is also used as detector in gas chromatography.

Kelvin, Baron (1824-1907)

He was a British Physicist Who Worked on electromagnetism and invented the mirror galvanometer. He introduced the concept of absolute zero and developed Kelvin based on this. The scale is named after him. He contributed to the development of telegraphy.

Kelvin scale

It is a temperature scale based on the concept of absolute zero which begins with it and increases by the same degree. In Kelvin scale, 0°C is 273K and 100°C is 373K. It is used in scientific measurement in the SI unit system.

Kapler' laws

The term is used for the three laws of planetary motion formulated by Johannes Kapler which are: (i) the orbit of the planets are elliptical with the sun at one focus; (ii) the planet orbits the sun so that an imaginary line between a planet and the sun sweeps out the equal areas in equal time; and (iii) the squares of the two periods of any two planets are proportional to the cubes of their major orbital axes.

Keratin

The term is used for the fibrous proteins present in hair, skin, nail, claws, feathers, and horns in vertebrates.

Keyboard

It is an input device in computer, very much like the keyboard in the typewriter, but many more variations in layout and labelling of keys as well.

Keyboard

Kidney

It is a pea-shaped organ in vertebrates which is a major organ of excretion of waste materials from the body. It filters waste in the body and remove it as urine. There are a pair of kidneys in vertebrates each one of them is made up of minute tubules called nephrons. These nephrons filter the waste and lead them to the ureter and bladder.

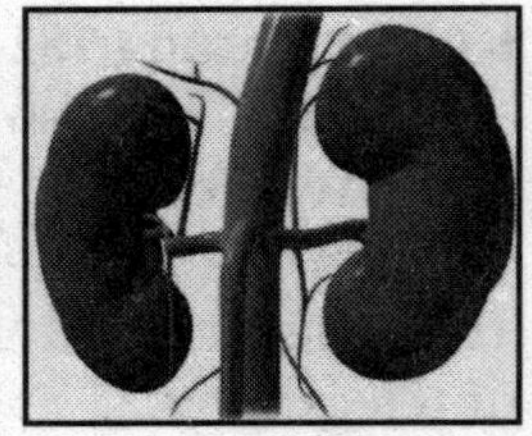

Kidney

Kilo (*Symbol* k)

It is a prefix used in metric system to denote 1000, e.g. kilogram, kilovolt, etc.

Kilowatt-hour (*Symbol* kWh)

It can be defined as a work done when a rate of work of thousand watt is maintained for one hour (1 Wh = 3.6×10^{16} joules). It is the commercial unit of electrical energy.

Kimberlite

It is form of rare igneous rock which contains mica, calcite, serpentine and other minerals. It is abundantly found in Kimberly in South Africa and is named after it.

Kinematics

It is the branch of mechanics which studies motion without any concern with the force causing it unlike dynamics which studies the forces affecting the motion.

Kinetics

It refers to a branch of chemistry which studies the rate of chemical reactions to determine the mechanism of reactions.

Kingdom

It represents the largest category of organisms classification. Originally, there were classification which now have been increased to five: (i) kingdom platae; (ii) kingdom animalia; (iii) kingdom protista ; (iv) kingdom fungi; and (v) kingdom monera.

Kipp's apparatus

The term refers to the laboratory apparatus used for making gases, e.g. CO_2, H_2, etc. It consists of three interconnected vertically arranged glass globes, with the solid in the central globe.

Klin

It is a furnace or oven used for firing clay and for various other purposes such as roasting sulphide ores, removing carbon dioxide from limestone, etc.

Klinostat

It is a device used in experiment to test the influence of growth on the growth of plants.

Knot

It is a unit of navigation which shows the speed of a ship. One knot is equivalent to one nautical mile per hour. It is used in aviation too (1 knot = 1.15 miles per hour).

Krebs, Sir Hans Adolf (1900-81)

He was born in Germany but later took British nationality and worked at Sheffield University and later moved to Oxford in 1954. Krebs is best known for the Krebs cycle. He was awarded the Nobel Prize for Medicine with Fritz Lipmann in 1953.

Krebs, Sir Hans Adolf

Krebs cycle

It is a cyclic sequence of biochemical reactions which is fundamental to the metabolism of organisms. The cycle is operated by the enzymes in the mitochondria.

Krypton (*Symbol* Kr)

It is a colourless inert gaseous element of group 0 of the periodic table, atomic number 36; atomic weight 83.8; melting point 156.6°C; boiling point –153.22. It is a noble gas used in fluorescent lamps.

Kwashiorkor

It is a deficiency disease common in tropics, largely affecting the infants and the young children. It is caused by protein deficiency with symptoms like anaemia, oedema, fatty liver, etc. If not treated, the child can die.

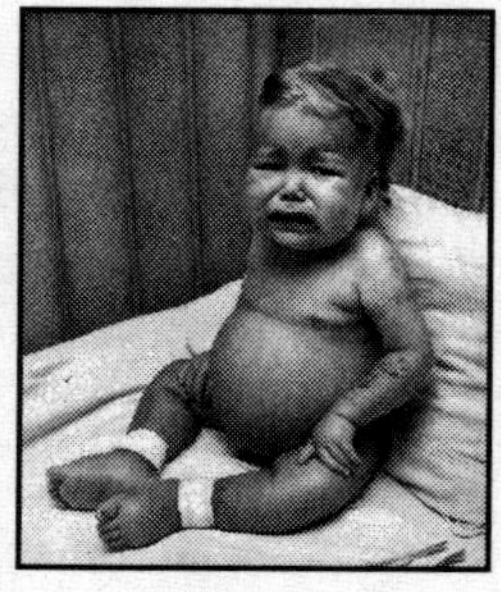

Kwashiorkor

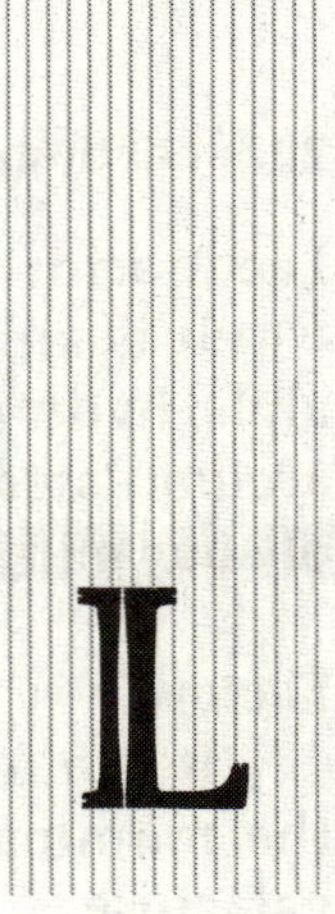

L

Labelling

It means replacing an atom in a compound with a radioisotope of the same element so as to enable its path through a biological or mechanical system by tracing the radiation that it emits. This process is very useful in biology, medicine and engineering.

Labium

The term refers to the lower lips in the mouthparts of insects.

Labyrinth

It includes the whole system of inner ear invertebrates, including cavities and tubes.

Lacrimal gland

It is a small gland in the eye of a vertebrate which secretes salty substance that helps to protect eyes from dust and other external agents.

Lacrimal gland

Lactase

It is an enzyme which catalyses the hydrolysis of lactose to glucose and galactose.

Lactation

It means the secretion of milk in the mammary glands, generally occurring after the birth of the young ones to feed them.

Lactic acid

It is an odourless organic acid present in milk. It is an alpha hydroxyl carboxylic acid. During exercise lactic acid gets accumulated in muscles and causes pain. It is a characteristic of sour milk. It is used in tanning and dying.

Lactose

It is a form of sugar present in milk. It is produced by the mammary glands. It is converted into glucose and galactose.

Lanolin

It is a emulsion of purified wool fat containing terpene alcohols and esters. It is used in cosmetics, and in leather industry.

Lanthanoids (lanthanides, lanthanons)

The term includes a series of 15 very reactive, silvery metallic elements, often called rare earths. They have common chemical properties and they usually occur together.

Laparoscopy

The term is used for an endoscopic examination of the body with the help of a tube-shaped instrument which is put through the abdominal wall. It is done for biopsy, etc.

Larva

It is the very early stage in the life cycle of most invertebrates, fish, amphibians, etc. when it has just come out of an egg and look like a short form of the adult one. Larvae are self-supporting and they develop into adults by undergoing metamorphosis.

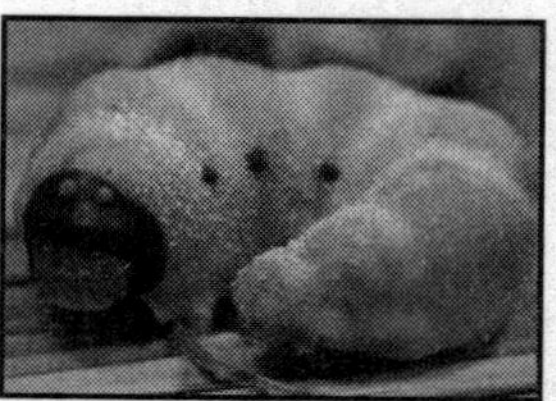

Larva

LASER

It is an abbreviation for Light Amplification by Stimulated Emission of Radiation. It is used as a device to produce very intense monochromatic electromagnetic radiation. Lasers may be solid, liquid or gas devices. It is used in surgery, printing, welding and holography.

Laser printer

It refers to a laser printer in which images are formed by a laser on a photosensitive drum and then transferred to paper to be printed. It works on a xerographic technique in which a low power laser is used to scan a photosensitive plate.

Laser printer

Laser surgery

It is an advanced technology in which an intense narrow beam of radiation is used to cut tissues in the human body. It is widely used in eye surgery.

Latent period

The term is used for that short period of time which goes by between the reception of a stimulus and the subsequent response. Usually, for a contracting muscle it lasts about 0.02 seconds.

Latex

It is a plant secretion consisting of resins and proteins. It is a milky substance produced by plants like poppy, rubber, etc. The latex of rubber has various commercial uses.

Lathe

It is a machine used for giving shapes to pieces of wood or metals by holding and turning them against a fixed cutting tool. It is moved by electric motors.

Laughing gas (*Symbol* N_2O)

It is a sweet-smelling colourless gas, nitrous oxide, used as an anaesthetic in minor surgery.

Laxative

It refers to a medicine which helps in constipation by emptying their bowels, e.g. Epsom salt.

LCD

Abbreviation for Liquid Crystal Display, it is a flat panel display, used with computers, other digital instruments and TV. LCD technology is based on liquid crystals in which electric current is passed through a special liquid and numbers and images can be seen on a screen.

LCD TV

Lead (*Symbol* Pb)

It is a soft, grey, ductile element of group 14 (formerly IV B) of the periodic table, atomic number: 82; atomic weight 207.19; melting point 327.4°C; boiling point 1740°C. Lead is widely used in building construction, bullet and shots, and also in lead alloys.

Leclanche cell

It is a primary voltaic cell consisting of a positive electrode of carbon and a zinc rod dipped into an electrolyte of ammonium chloride. It gives an emf of 1.5 volts. The widely used dry cells in torches, transistor sand calculators are based on this.

Legume

The term refers to dry fruits formed of a single carpel, characteristic fruit of plants of Leguminosae family, e.g. peas, beans, etc. which split when they are mature. Their roots have nitrogen fixing bacteria which add to the soil fertility.

Lens

The term is used for a transparent optical element with either a convex or concave surface, for diverging or converging the transmitted light to form an image. Lens are used in binoculars, optical instruments, telescopes, microscopes, etc.

Leprosy

It is a contagious disease, caused by a bacteria *Mycobacterium leprae*, commonly seen in tropical countries. It affects skin, bones, nerves and muscles.

Leptotene

It is the first substage of prophase in meiosis, when the chromosomes contract and become visible as two fine chromatids.

Leucocyte

It refers to a colourless cell present in blood and lymph, etc. They are formed in lymph nodes and red bone marrow and fight against foreign bodies. Thus, they protect from diseases.

Leukemia

It is a serious disease in which excess leucocytes are produced in blood by bone marrow and other organs which leads to susceptibility to infection, anaemia, weakness and bleeding. Sometimes symptoms include enlargement of liver, spleen, lymph nodes. Leukemia is treated with radiotherapy or cytotoxic drugs.

Lever

It is a simple machine with a rigid bar pivoted about a fulcrum. There are three orders of a lever, each one has a different mechanical advantage.

Lever

Lichens

The term represents a symbiotic dissociation of fungus and green algae, commonly seen on rocks, plants, etc.

Lie detector

It is an instrument which presents graphical records of certain activities like respiration, pulse, blood pressure. It is used in investigation of criminal cases to find out false answers of the criminals.

Life cycle

It presents a complete sequence of developmental stages in the life of an organism.

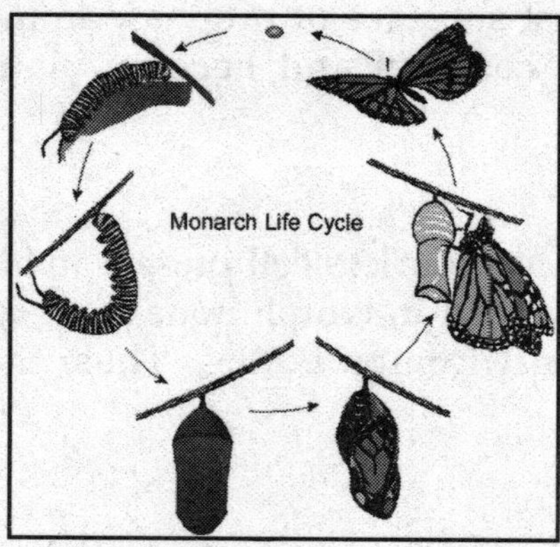

Life cycle

Life expectancy

The term can be defined as the average number of years that a person is likely to live. Recently, as a result of advancement in the field of science and technology, it has increased.

Light

It is a form of electromagnetic wave sensitive to the human eyes with the wavelength from 380-780 nm.

Lightning

It is a high-energy electrical discharge passing between charged clouds or charged cloud and earth, producing a flash or flashes. Usually, it is followed by thunder.

Light year

It is defined as the distance travelled by light in a year, i.e. 300000 km or 9.46 trillion km. It is a unit of distance used in astronomy.

Lignite

It is an inferior variety of coal intermediate between bituminous coal and peat. It has low carbon content and is used as fuel.

Limewater

It is a saturated solution of calcium hydroxide in water.

Limnology

It relates to the scientific study of lakes and other fresh water sources including their flora and fauna, and their properties.

Linear motor

It is a type of induction motor in which the stator and armature are linear and parallel. Due to cost and efficiency factors, the motor does not have much commercial viability.

Linear motor

Lipase

It is an enzyme produced by the pancreas which breaks down fat into fatty acid and glycerol.

Lipid

It refers to any of the organic compounds, soluble in alcohol and insoluble in water, e.g. esters of fatty acids, steroids and terpenes.

Liquefaction

It refers to the conversion of gases into a liquid under low/high temperature but very high pressure. Liquefied petroleum gas and liquefied natural gas are the examples of liquefaction.

Liquid

It refers to a phase of matter which can flow easily and takes the shape of the vessel that contains it. Liquids do not have any shape.

Liquid crystals

The term is used for a substance which flows like liquid but has both liquid and solid properties because the molecules are arranged in some order. This arrangement can be changed by electric or magnetic field. Liquid crystals are used in watches, calculators thermometers, etc.

Lithium

It is a soft silvery, metal in group 1 (formerly IA) of the periodic table; atomic number 3; atomic weight 6.94; melting point 180.6°C; boiling point 1342°C. It is an alkali metal with low density. The metal is used to harden alloys, in batteries and in medicine as well.

Litre (*Symbol* L or l)

It is a metric unit of volume, formerly defined as the volume occupied by 1 kilogram of pure water at 4°C at standard pressure.

Liver

It is large organ situated in the abdomen of the vertebrates which serves as a regulating and storage organ. It converts glucose to store as glycogen, breaks down fats, removes waste products, synthesises vitamins, secretes bile, etc.

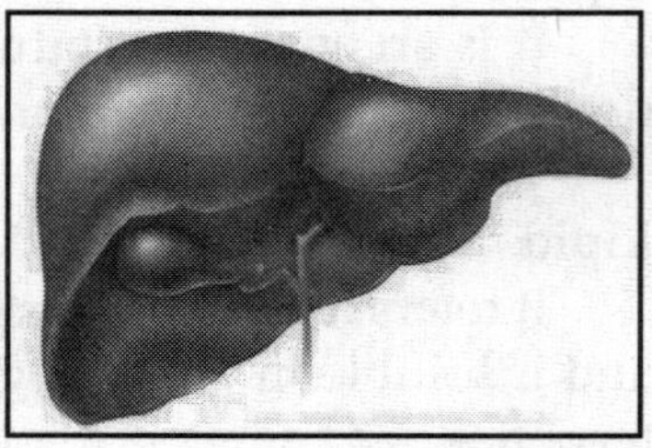

Liver

Locomotion

It can be defined as the ability of an organism to move from one place to another, primarily for food and mating.

Lung

It is a pair of respiratory organ, consisting of thin moist membrane situated in the thorax in vertebrates. The exchange of gases takes place in lungs. The process of respiration involves both inspiration and expiration.

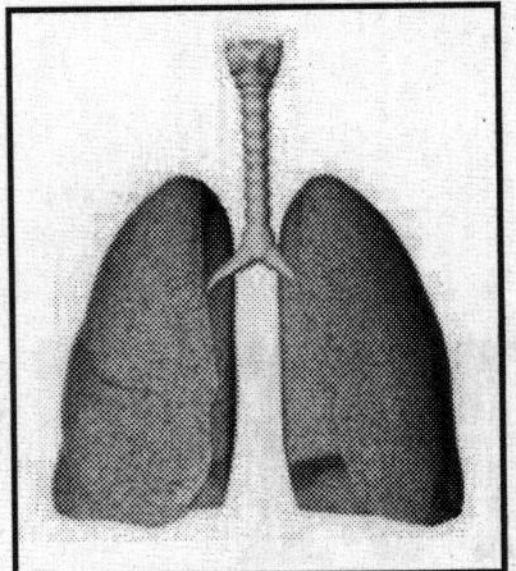

Lungs

Lux (*Symbol* lx)

It is the SI unit of illuminance. It is equal to one lumen per square meter.

❑

Machine

It is a device which makes mechanical work easier by overcoming the force of resistance. It uses energy to perform work. Lever, wedge, wheel and axle are the examples of simple machine.

Macronutrient

The term refers to an element which is required in large quantity for the proper growth, good and development and for good health. This includes phosphorous, calcium, magnesium, nitrogen, etc.

It is a trade name for an aluminium-based alloy which contains 5-30% magnesium and 29-95% aluminium. The metal is highly reflective of the ultraviolet radiation and light, hence used in the manufacturing of aircraft.

Magnet

It is a piece of magnetic material, usually iron, with magnetic properties, i.e. attraction, repulsion and magnetic field. A magnet is often in the shape of a bar or horse shoe. Magnets are two types – permanent and temporary.

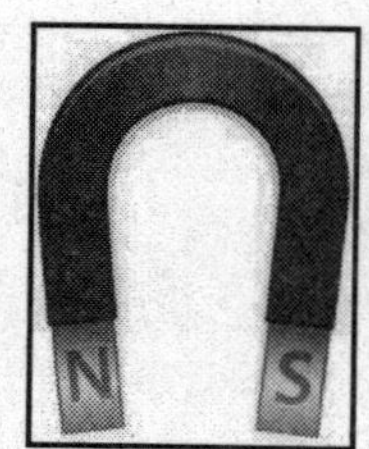

Magnet

Magnetic Resonance Imaging(MRI)

It is a scanning process used medical, particularly in the diagnosis of brain and spinal problems. It is based on the principles of nuclear magnetic resonance and gives three-dimensional images of tissues being scanned without causing pain and radiation.

Magnetite

It is black iron ore or mineral form of iron which is strongly magnetic. It is found in igneous or metamorphic rock. Some of its varieties like loadstones behave like magnet.

Magnetometer

It is an instrument used for measuring magnitude and direction of a magnetic field.

Malaria

It is a tropical disease caused by the protozoa *Plasmodium* and transmitter by *Anopheles* mosquitoes. Its symptoms include high fever accompanied with shivering and anaemia. Quinine and chloroquine is used to treated the disease.

Malleability

It refers to the property of a metal to be hit and pressed into a thin sheet without cracking or breaking. Metals like gold, silver, copper, etc. have high malleability.

Malnutrition

It denotes a poor state of health caused by inadequate supply of proper food making the victim unhealthy and weak.

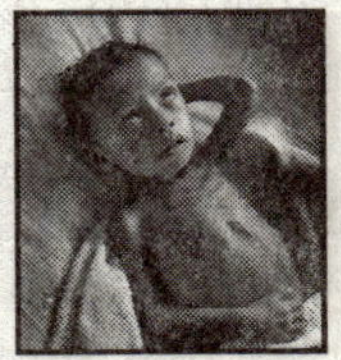

Malnutrition

Mammography

The term is used for the medical examination of breast using X-rays or infrared rays for finding any abnormal growth of tissues.

Manometer

It is a device used for measuring pressure differences in fluids. It consists of a U-tube with water or coloured liquid and a tap.

Marsh gas

It is a gas produced in the marshes by the decay of plants. It mainly consists of methane largely found in marshy places. It is highly combustible.

MASER

It is the abbreviated form of Microwave Amplification by Stimulated Emission of Radiation. It is a device used to amplify or generate microwave by means of stimulated emission. It is a high-frequency microwave amplifier. It is used in atomic clocks and radio astronomy.

Mass extinction

It means total removal of a species from the earth within a relatively short interval of geological time scale, e.g. dinosaurs in the Mesozoic age. The fossil record provides evidence for mass extinction.

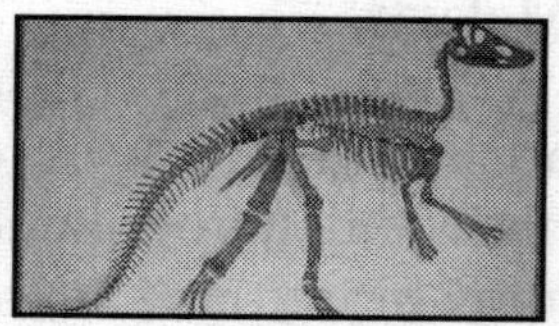

Mass extinction

Measles

It is a virus disease largely affecting children. It is highly infectious with incubation period of 7-14 days. Specific treatment is available.

Mechanics

It is a branch of Physical Science which studies interactions between matter and the forces which cause the motions, including the forces acting on bodies in a state of equilibrium.

Melting point

It is the point at which a substance melts or turns into a liquid. All pure substances have some definite melting temperature. During melting, temperature remains unchanged.

Mercury (*Symbol* Hg)

It is a heavy silvery metallic element, found in liquid state, belonging to zinc group, atomic number 80; atomic wight 220.59;

melting point – 38.82°C; boiling point 356.73°C. Mercury is a poisonous element. Its main ore is cinnabar (HgS). It is used in thermometers, barometers, and other scientific devices, and dentistry.

Metabolism

The chemical processes in organisms which change food into energy and materials for growth. It includes all the chemical processes from growth to functions. It involves both building up processes and the breaking down.

Metal

It is a class of chemical element which is usually hard and lustrous and is a good conductor of heat and electricity. Though these properties are not present in all metals, e.g. mercury is a liquid.

Metallurgy

It refers to a branch of applied science which deals with metals, alloys and the processes of their production and purification.

Metallurgy

Meteorology

It concerns the study of the physical phenomena and processes taking place in earth's atmosphere, e.g. weather and climate. The study of meteorology has great importance for the navigation of ships and aircraft.

Methane

It is a colourless, odourless gas and the simplest hydrocarbon. Also called marsh gas, it is the main constituent of natural gas and the basis of many organic compounds. It is used as a fuel.

Mica

It refers to a group of silicate minerals found in layers. Mica is used as electrical insulator.

Micrometer

It is a device for accurately measuring small diameters, thickness, etc.

Micron

It is a unit for measuring length, equal to one millionth of a meter (10^{-6}m). It is the SI unit for micrometer.

Microphone

It is a device which converts sound energy into electrical energy.

Microscope

It is a scientific instrument which forms magnified image of very small objects or organisms. A compound microscope consists of two convex lenses of short focal length while a simple one has a biconvex magnifying glass, either hand held or in a simple frame.

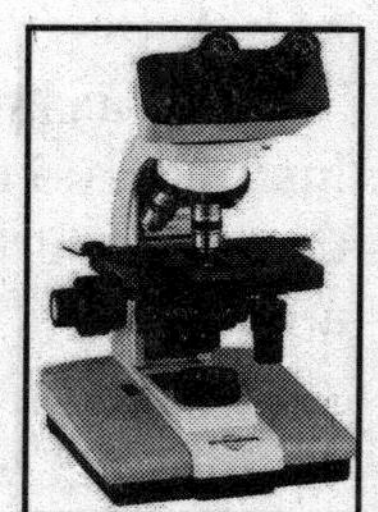

Microscope

Microwaves

The term is used for electromagnetic radiation which is shorter than a radio wave but longer than a light wave, in the range of 1 mm to 30 cm. Microwaves are used as carrier waves in telecommunication, satellite communication, etc.

Milli- (*Symbol* m)

Used in metric system, it is a prefix used to denote one 1000 or 10^{-3}, e.g. millimetre (10^{-3} m).

Mineral

It is a naturally occurring crystalline inorganic substance. Usually, minerals are solid, but some of them are liquid or gas as well, e.g. oil, natural gas, etc.

Mirror

The term is used for an optical element which reflects most of the light that falls on it. There are different types of mirror, for example, plane mirror, spherical mirrors, concave or convex mirror.

Modem

It is a device which converts digital signal into an analogue signal or vice versa. Hence, modems are used to connect one computer system to another using a telephone line.

Modem

Moderator

It is a material or substance which slows down free neutrons in a nuclear reactor and thus prevents nuclear explosion. Heavy water, graphite, cadmium are the examples of moderators.

Mohs' scale

It is a scale in which a series of ten metals are arranged in order of their hardness. It is used to measure the hardness of the metals. The order of arrangement of metals is: talc, gypsum, calcite, fluorite, apatite orthoclase, quartz, topaz, corundum, diamond. This scale was devised by Friedrich Mohs (1773-1839).

Molecule

It is one of the fundamental units of compound as well as the smallest part of a chemical compound which can take part in a chemical reaction. It consists of one or more free atoms.

Morphology

It refers to the scientific study of the external structure and form of plants and animals.

Motor

It is device which converts chemical energy or electrical energy into chemical energy, e.g. internal combustion engine, electric motor, etc.

Moulting

The term can be defined as the periodical shedding of skin, epidermis, cuticles or horns, in arthropods, e.g. snakes.

Muscle

The term refers to bundles of cells or fibres attached to bones. They are contractile and reflexive in nature and produce tension and movement in the body. Muscles are voluntary and involuntary.

Muscle

Myopia

It is an eye defect in which a person cannot see things clearly when they are far away because the image is formed before the retina. The condition can be corrected by using a concave lens to move the image back to the retina.

❑

N

It is used as a symbol for nitrogen and Newton.

Nano- (*Symbol* n)

It is a prefix in the metric system to denote one thousand millionth, i.e. 10^{-9}, e.g. 1 nanogram = 10^{-9} gram.

Nanotechnology

It is the branch of Science which studies structures which are less than 100 nanometres long. These structures are often built with the help of individual molecules of substances. It is also used for the development and use of devices which are only a few nanometers in size.

Nanotechnology

Narcotic

It refers to a powerful drug that affects the mind in a harmful way. Narcotics are addictive and they cause dependency. Narcotics are used to relieve pain. Its medical use is strictly controlled.

Natural gas

It refers to a mixture of gaseous hydrocarbons largely found in the sedimentary rocks under the ground of the earth usually with oil deposits. It mainly consists of methane, ethane, butane and propane. It is used as fuel.

Nautical mile

It is a measure of distance at sea which is 6080 feet or 1852 meters by international definition.

Neon (*Symbol* Ne)

It is a gaseous element belonging to group 1 of the periodic table (the noble gases), atomic number 10; atomic weight 20.179; melting point – 248.59°C; boiling point – 246.08°C. Neon is present in air (0.0018%) and is used in discharge tubes and neon lamps.

Nephron

The term is used for the filtering unit of kidney which consists of a Bowman's capsule and a glomerulus in which constituents of blood are filtered. The waste material like salts, water, etc. gather in the Bowman's capsule and the filtered fluids are reabsorbed in the surrounding blood capillaries.

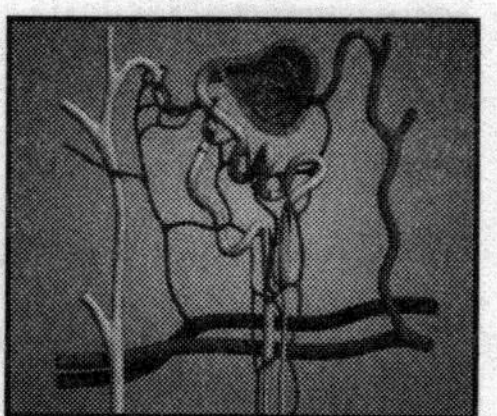

Nephron

Nerve

The term is used for a strand of tissue consisting of many nerve fibres and supporting tissues, enclosed in a sheath of connective tissue. Nerves connect the organs and nervous system and carry sensory or motor impulses. There are different kinds of nerves such as sensory nerves, motor nerves and mixed nerves. All nerves are part of the nervous system.

Nerve gas

The term is used for a group of toxic gases which are esters of fluorophosphoric acid. They are used in warfare because they attack the central nervous system.

Nervous system

The term includes tissues, nerves, nerve fibres and other parts which convey information between sensory cells and organs as well as muscles and glands, and interprets and coordinates all systems. The nervous system controls all the function of the body and formulates responses according to the information received.

Neuron

It is the fundamental unit of the nervous system which consists of a cell body containing the nucleus, dendrites and axons and nissl granules. It is an elongated branched cell which is specialised for conducting impulses.

Neuron

Neuron

It is one of the basic particles in an atom which is unstable outside the nucleus. It has a mass of about 1.675×10^{-27} kg with no charge. A normal hydrogen atom has no neutron in it. Neutron was discovered by James Chadwick in 1932.

Neutron bomb

It is a kind of small nitrogen bomb based on fission-fusion reaction in which most of the energy is released as high energy neutrons. This neutron radiation is very harmful to people.

Niacin

It is a vitamin of B-complex group, present in plants and animals. Deficiency of niacin causes pellagra.

Nichrome

It is an alloy of nickel (80%) and chromium (20%) which has high resistance to oxidation and melting point. It is used for wires in heating elements.

Nickel (*Symbol* Ni)

It is a hard silvery metallic element atomic number 28; atomic weight: 58.70; melting point 1450°C; boiling point: 2732°C. Nickel is found in igneous rocks in the minerals pentlandite, pyrrhoite, and garnierite. Nickel is used in steels, magnetic alloys, and as a catalyst.

Night blindness

It refers to a condition in which a person suffers from poor night vision. It is caused by the deficiency of vitamin A. It is caused by a defect in rods of the retina.

Nitrification

It is a chemical process in which nitrogen in plants and animal wastes is oxidized to nitrites and then to nitrates. This is brought about by nitrifying bacteria *Nitrosomonas* and *Nitrobacter*. It is an important part of nitrogen cycle.

Nitrogen cycle

It refers to the cyclic circulation of nitrogen and nitrogenous compounds between various organisms and plants. Nitrates present in the soils are absorbed by plant root and are passed to animals through food chain. Compounds which contain nitrogen are decomposed by specialised bacteria into nitrates which are again used by plants. Atmospheric nitrogen is assimilated by nitrogen fixing bacteria which again goes to plants. Lightning also contributes to the formation of oxides of nitrogen which enter the soil. Thus, it makes acycle.

Nitrogen cycle

Nitroglycerine

It is a pale yellow oily liquid which explodes violently on the slight shock. It is an ester of nitric acid. It is used in dynamites.

Noble gases

The term is used for group O elements or gases in group VIII A of the periodic table. These gases are neon, helium, krypton, argon and xenon. Chemically, these gases are inert and are present in air at only trace level. They are also called rare gases.

Noble metals

The term refers to metals which are not corroded by acids. Noble metals have great value. Gold, silver, platinum, iridium, etc. are examples of noble metals.

Nocturnal

It means related to or happening during the night. A nocturnal animal is active only during the night, e.g. bats, owl, etc.

Non-conductor

The term is used for the materials which act as insulator. They do not allow the flow of heat, electricity or sound, e.g. rubber, plastic, etc.

Non-metals

It refers to an element which is not a metal and they are either insulators or semiconductors. They are neither ductile nor malleable. They are poor conductor of heat or electricity. Carbons, oxygen, sulphur, phosphorous, etc. are the examples of non-metals.

Nuclear energy

Nuclear energy

It refers to the energy generated by nuclear fission or nuclear fusion. The fission of one uranium atom produces about 3.2×10^{-11} joules while the combustion of one carbon atom yields about 6.4×10^{-19} joule. Uranium generates about 2500000 times more energy than carbon combustion.

Nuclear fuel

The term is used for a substance which can sustain a fission chain reaction to be used as a source of nuclear energy. Uranium-233, uranium-235, plutonium-239, plutonium-241 are the examples of nuclear fuel.

NMR

Abbreviation for nuclear magnetic resonance, it is a type of radio frequency spectroscopy. It is based on the magnetic field generated by the spin of atomic nuclei which are electrically charged. It is used medical for diagnosis purposes.

Nuclear reactor

It is a huge structure in which nuclear energy is produced by sustained and controlled chain reaction using nuclear fuels such as uranium-235, plutonium-239 and uranium-233.

Nuclear weapons

The term includes explosion devices in which explosion is caused by nuclear fission, nuclear fusion or by both. Nuclear bomb, hydrogen bomb, neutron bomb, etc. are the examples of nuclear bombs. They are weapons of mass destruction.

Nuclear weapons

Nylon

The term is used for various synthetic polyamide which has a protein-like structure. Nylon is formed by the condensation of one amino group of one molecule and a carboxylic group of another.

❑

Obstetrics

It is a branch of Medicine concerned with the care of the pregnancy including allied problems and birth of the children.

Oedema

It refers to a condition in which liquid collects in tissues or organs leading to swelling. It is actually a symptoms of diseases related to liver, kidney or heart.

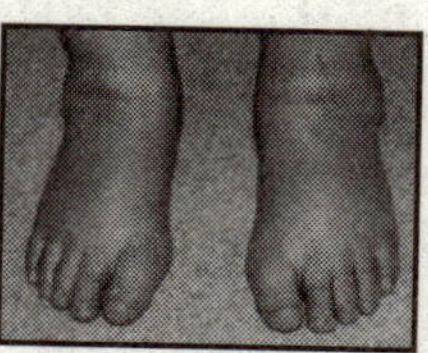

Oedema

Oersted (*Symbol* Oe)

It is the unit of magnetic field strength in the cgs system, now replaced by the SI unit ampere per meter. It is named after Hans Oersted.

Oestrogen

The term includes a group of sex hormones mainly produced by the ovaries which promotes secondary sexual character in females and controls menstrual cycle in them. They are used in contraceptives and also in the treatment of various diseases in females.

Ohm (*Symbol* &!)

It is the derived SI unit of electrical resistance. It is named after Georg Ohm.

Omnivorous

It refers to animals which eat all types of food including plants and animals.

Oncology

It relates to the scientific study and treatment of tumours in the body.

Open-hearth process

It is an old method of manufacturing steel, now replaced by basic oxygen process. In this process, scrap, pig iron and hot metal are heated together in an open furnace using heat produced by burning producer gas in air.

Ophthalmology

It refers to the scientific study of eyes and related diseases including the anatomy and physiology.

Optic nerve

It is a large nerve consisting of millions of nerve fibres which carry visual impulses from the eye to the brain.

Optics

It is a branch of Physics which studies light and sight, for example Mirror, lenses, microscopes, telescopes, etc. including the related phenomena like reflection, refraction, dispersion, etc.

Oral contraceptive

It is a medicine taken orally to prevent a woman from becoming pregnant. It contains hormones like oestrogen and progesterone which suppress ovulation in women.

Oral contraceptive

Organ

It refers to a part of an organism specialised to perform a particular function or functions, for example – eyes, heart, kidneys in animals and leaves, roots, etc. in plants.

Organic

The term is used for the substances related to living organisms or compound which contain carbon.

Organic chemistry

It is the branch of Chemistry concerning carbon compounds.

Organism

The term refers to an individual living system which is capable of growth, reproduction and maintenance. Plants, animals and microorganisms are the examples of organism.

Orthopaedics

It is the branch of medicine concerned with the injuries and diseases of bones and muscles, including related deformities caused by disease or damage.

Oscillator

It is an electronic device which produces sonic or ultrasonic pressure waves which keep changing its strength and direction in a medium to produce desired oscillation.

Osteomalacia

It refers to a condition in which bones become soft. It is caused by the deficiency of vitamin D. It is treated with vitamin D and calcium.

Ostrich

It is a very bird with a long neck and long legs, found mainly in Africa. It lays big eggs and cannot fly.

Otter

It is a four-legged carnivorous mammal found in Asia and Europe. It lives in rivers and feeds on sea animals like fish, frogs, etc. It is a good swimmer.

Otter

Ovary

It is the reproductive organ in female where ova are produced. The organ also produces hormones like oestrogen and progesterone. In most vertebrates there is a pair of ovaries which contain follicles in which ova develop and later released regularly in menstrual cycle.

Ovule

It is a part of the female reproductive organ in seed plants which consists of nucellus, embryo sac and integuments. After fertilization, the ovule turns into seeds.

Oxygen (Symbol O)

It is a colourless, odourless gaseous element in group 16 of the periodic table (formerly VI B) atomic number 8; atomic weight 15.99; melting point – 218.79°C; boiling points – 182.9°C. It is the most abundantly found element in the earth's crust (42.9%) and in atmosphere it constitutes about 28% by volume. Oxygen was discovered by Joseph Priestly in 1774.

Oxygen cycle

It is a cyclical process of taking in oxygen from, and giving out to the environment where it happens as respiration in human beings and animals, and as photosynthesis in plants.

Ozone layer

It refers to a layer in the earth's atmosphere at 20-40 km altitude where ozone is in high concentration and absorbs much of the ultraviolet radiation in sunlight thus preventing it from reaching to the earth's surface. The radiation are harmful to the organisms. It acts as a protective layer.

Ozone layer

❑

P

It is a symbol for proton, phosphorous, protactinum.

Pacemaker

It denotes the following:

1. It refers to a group of specialised muscle cells in the wall of the mammalian heart which maintain the heart beat and are controlled by the autonomous nervous system.
2. It is an electronic device planted surgically into the chest to support the heart beat when natural pacemaker does not work properly.

Paediatrics

It is the branch of study concerned with the study of children and their diseases.

Pancreas

It is an organ in vertebrates located in the abdominal cavity which secretes pancreatic juice that helps in digestion. Besides, the group of cells in the pancreas, called the islets of Langerhans and functions as endocrine gland. It produces insulin and glucagon which regulates sugar level in blood.

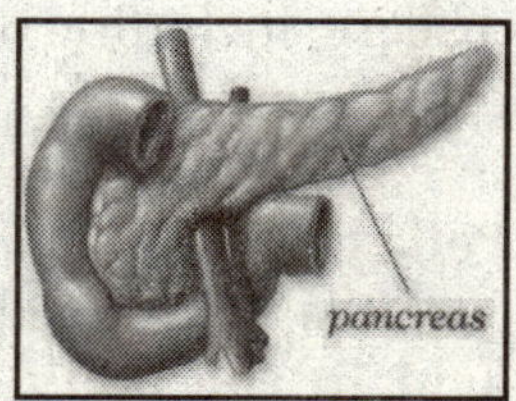

Pancreas

Pandemic

It refers to a disease which spreads across all region in a country or the whole world, e.g. influenza.

Parasite

The term refers to an organism which feeds on other plants or organisms called host. This relationship is not good for the host.

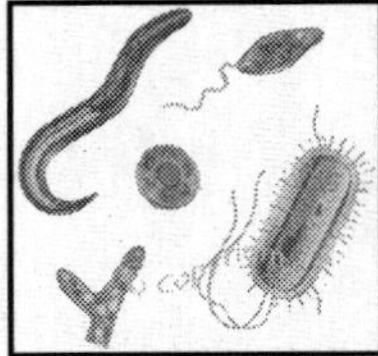

Parasite

Parkinson's disease

It is a chronic disease which affects brain and voluntary actions. Its symptoms include tremors, trembling of hands, shaking of head, stiffness, weak muscles, etc. medication helps in checking the symptoms.

Pascal (*Symbol* Pa)

It is the SI unit of pressure which is equal to one newton per square meter.

Pasteurisation

It refers to the treatment of milk to destroy the harmful bacteria in it. For the treatment, milk is first heated to 65°C for 30 minutes or to 72°C for 15 minutes then it is rapidly cooled to below 10°C. This method was devised by French Bacteriologist Louis Pasteur.

Pathology

It is the branch of Medicine concerned with the study of disease, including diagnosis by examining body fluids, tissues, organs, etc.

Pellagra

It is a chronic disease caused by the deficiency of nicotine acid in the body. Its symptoms include diarrhoea, skin eruptions, neuritis, anaemia, mental disturbances, and ataxia. The disease is common in subtropical countries.

Penicillin

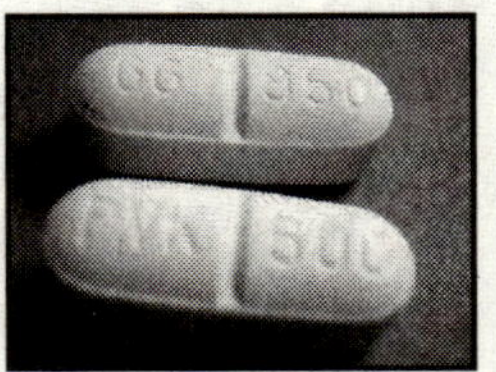
Penicillin

It is a group of antibiotic derived from the mould *Penicillium notatum*, also known as Penicillin G. Discovered by Sir Alexander Fleming, the antibiotic is active against a variety of disease but it is in effective in viral infection.

Pesticide

The term is used for a chemical substance that kills harmful insects, and organisms and pests, e.g. pyrethrum, Paraquat, DDT, etc. Some pesticides are persistent and not easily biodegradable, hence harmful for the environment.

Petroleum

It is a highly inflammable mineral oil found in sedimentary rocks under the ground. It is a mixture of hydrocarbons formed in ages under the heat and pressure under the ground. Petroleum products are used in manufacturing of a variety of things like detergent, plastics, insecticides, fertilizers, pharmaceuticals, etc. The superior quality of petroleum is used in aviation.

pH

It is the measurement of the level of acidity and alkalinity in a solution which is actually the concentration of hydrogen ions in the solution. The scale is marked from 0 to 14 in which a reading of 7 pH indicates neutrality, below is acidic and above 7 is alkaline.

Pharmacology

The term is used the study and properties of the drugs, their use in medicine and their effect on living organisms.

Photometer

It is an instrument used measuring the luminous intensity and other photometric quantities.

Photosynthesis

It is a chemical process in which green plants synthesise organic compounds, namely carbohydrates and water in the presence of sunlight, occurring in chloroplasts. Photosynthesis forms the basis of all life on earth. Also the presence of oxygen in the environment is due to photosynthesis as the oxygen is released during the process.

Pitchblende

It is the chief ore of uranium, containing radium, polonium, thorium and helium apart from uranium.

Pituitary gland

It refers to an endocrine gland located in the brain. This pea-shaped gland produces many hormones which control growth and function of other hormones in the body.

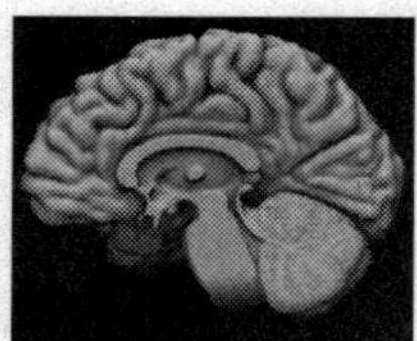

Pituitary gland

Pollution

The term refers to the harmful changes caused to the environment by various human activities such as industrialisation, urbanisation, deforestation, etc. Industries produce huge amount of wastes that go air, water and soil and bring changes in their biological, physical and chemical characteristics. Besides, vehicles emit harmful substance which go into the environment and affect its quality. All these contribute to the pollution.

Power (*Symbol* P)

In Physics, it refers to the rate at which work is done or energy is transferred. Its SI unit is watts. In Mathematics it denotes the number of tomes a figure is multiplied, for example, x^8 means the eighth power of x.

Primary cell

It is a voltaic cell in which the emf produced as a result of chemical reaction is irreversible which means that the cell cannot be recharged by current.

Prism

Prism

It refers to a solid the ends of which are parallel and in same shape and size, with the sides of the opposite edges equal and parallel. Usually, it is triangular which deviates light ray or disperse it when it passes through it into colours of the rainbow.

Producer gas

It is a mixture of carbon monoxide and nitrogen produced by passing air over hot carbon. It is used as fuel in different industries.

Progesterone

It is a female sex hormone produced in the ovary after ovulation. It prepares the uterus to implant the zygote helps to maintain the pregnancy. It is also used as contraceptive.

Prosthesis

It refers to an artificial device used as a substitute to a defective or missing body part caused by disease or injury. Artificial limbs, false teeth and eyes, artificial pacemakers, artificial cardiac valves are all examples of prosthesis.

Protein

The term includes organic compounds present in all living things and is essential for the growth and maintenance of life. They are composed of hydrogen, carbon, oxygen, nitrogen, sulphur and phosphorus. Some proteins are soluble in water.

Pulley

It is a piece of simple equipment consisting of a wheel over which a chain or rope is pulled which makes it rotate about an axis. It is used for moving heavy objects up and down.

Pupa

It is the third stage in the development of life cycle in an insect which comes between larva and adult. In this stage, the insect is contained in a cocoon and cannot move or eat. In this stage, significant morphological changes take place inside pupa.

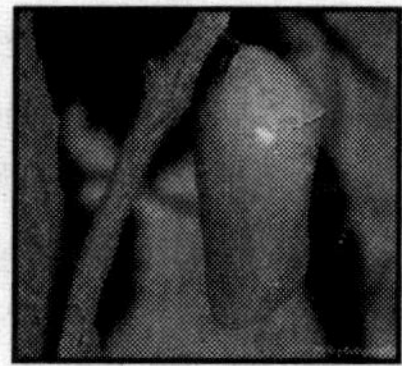

Pupa

❑

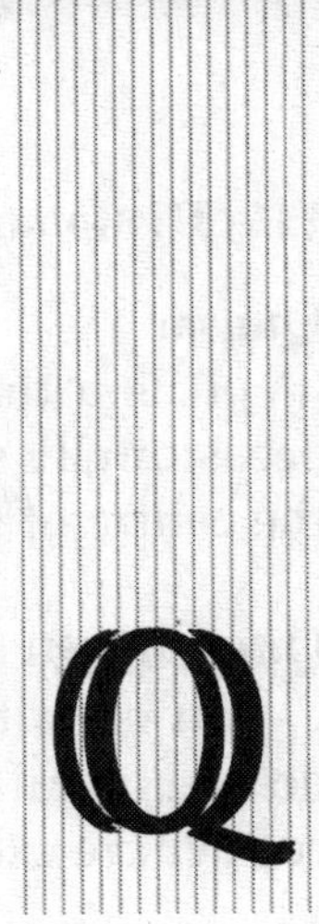

Quadrant

It is an instrument used to measure the altitude of stars. It was used in ancient time in astronomy and navigation.

Quadriplegia

It is a medical condition in which all four limbs are affected by paralysis.

Quadruple vaccine

It refers a vaccine which is a combination of four vaccines used for the treatment of pertussis, diphtheria, tetanus and poliomyelitis.

Quadruple vaccine

Quantum

It is the smallest amount of energy that a system can gain or lose. This concept makes the basis of quantum theory.

Quarantine

It refers to the period of time during which an individual suffering from communicable disease is kept separate to further avoid the spread of disease. Quarantine depends on the incubation period of the disease.

Quartz

It is a mineral found in rocks in different colours. Pure quartz is colourless and transparent while the impure varieties are used as gemstones, e.g. amethyst or agate.

Quasar

It is a distant large object, like a star which shines and occasionally sends out radio signals. They are believed to be the centre of galaxies producing large amount of energy.

Quenching

In metallurgy, the term refers to the rapid cooling of a heated metal mainly to make it harder, but some metals like copper are exception because they become soft on quenching.

Quinine

It is a medicine produced from the bark of the Cinchona tree. It is an effective medicine for the treatment of malaria. It is extremely bitter in taste.

Quinine

❑

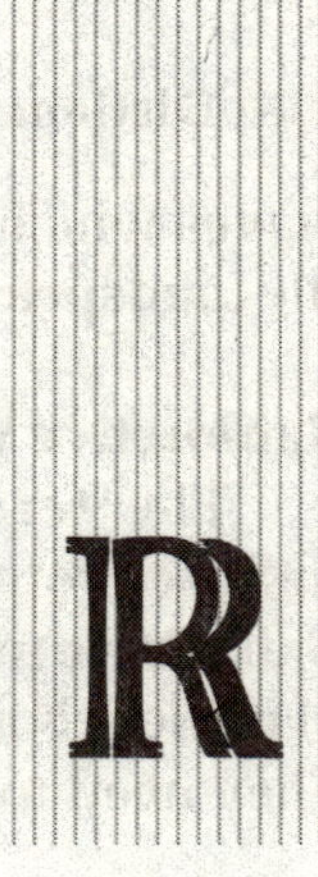

Rabies

It is a fatal disease caused by virus in human beings which affects the central nervous system. It is transmitted by a mad dog or other animal which enters the body when the animal bites. Symptoms include restlessness, muscle spasms, fear of water, etc. it is treated with a series injections containing weak rabies virus.

Rabies

Radar (Radio Detection and Ranging)

It is a method of detecting presence and position of a distant object like ships and aircraft with the help of transmitted and reflected high frequency electromagnetic radiation of centrimetric wavelengths. It is used in navigation, air traffic control and meteorology.

Radiation

It is a form of energy that comes out from a radioactive source, e.g. alpha or beta particles or from a nuclear reactor as neutron. Also a method of transfer of heat energy without any medium is called radiation.

Radio

It refers to a piece of electronic equipment used for transmission and reception of radiowaves. There is a microphone which converts sound waves into electromagnetic waves which are picked up by the receiving aerial and fed to the loudspeaker which converts it back into the sound waves.

Radioactive wastes

The term includes waste material which contains radioactive nuclide, usually coming out from the mining of radioactive material like pitch blende, nuclear reactors or fallout of nuclear bombs. They are hazardous to life and environment. They need to disposed of carefully.

Radio astronomy

The term is used for the study of radio frequency radiation emitted by celestial bodies, e.g. planets, galaxies, etc. using radio telescope.

Radio frequency

It is the range of frequencies between about 3 kilohertz and 300 gigahertz which is used in radio transmission for electromagnetic radiation.

Radio frequency

Radiology

It refers to the scientific study of different types of radiation, e.g. X-rays, gamma rays and other ionising radiations in medicine, particularly in the diagnosis and treatment of diseases.

Radiotherapy

It is a system of treatment in which cancerous or harmful tumours are treated with the help of X-rays, gamma rays or other waves. This can be done either by exposing the patient to radiation or by introducing them into the body by needle, e.g. radium needle.

Rain gauge

It is an instrument used to measure the rainfall over certain period of time, usually 24 hours.

Real gas

It refers to a gas which does not have the properties of real gas, its molecules have definite size and forces between them.

Receptor

The term is used for a special cell or group of cells which are sensitive to external stimuli and detects a stimulus and transmits it via sensory nerve. Sense organs like skin, eyes, ears, nose, etc. have receptors.

Red data book

It is a catalogue of species which are rare and endangered. In 1966, it was started by a Switzerland based organisation the International Union for Conservation of Nature and Natural Resources (IUCN).

Red Dwarf

The term refers to small, faint old star which is much cooler than the sun. It burns very slowly with a time span of about 100 billion years and display a number of magnetic phenomena.

Red Dwarf

Reflex

It is a natural uncontrollable reaction of the body in response to something, for example, a sudden withdrawal of hand in response to something hot touched. This is an involuntary automatic response.

Refraction

It refers to the change of direction that light or electromagnetic radiation suffers when it passes obliquely from one medium to another because the velocity of radiation changes when with the change in media.

Refrigerant

It is a liquid or gas which is volatile and easily liquefied and is used as a cooling agent in a refrigerator, for example, ammonia, sulphur dioxide, etc.

Remote sensing

It refers to the technique of gathering of information and data mainly about the earth without involving actual contact with the area under study, usually done by satellites. This is widely used in map-making.

Retina

It is the area at the back of the eye which is sensitive to light and sends signals to the brain about what has been. It consists of two layers.

Rickets

It is a disease common in children caused by the chronic deficiency of vitamin D or poor phosphate reabsorption in the body. Symptoms include softening of bones and deformity in them.

Robot

It is an electronic machine which can do all sorts of works, including work in dangerous situations like diffusing a bomb. It is controlled by computers. It is used in industry for doing various heavy works.

Robot

Roentgen rays

Named after the Scientist Wilhelm Conrad Roentgen, who discovered it, it refers to electromagnetic radiation of very short length. These rays are highly penetrating, hence used in medical science for diagnosis of diseases, besides many other uses.

Rubber

It is a mixture hydrocarbons obtained from the sap of the plant *Hevea brasiliensis*. It is a milky fluid which is obtained by taping its bark and then it is dried and vulcanised. This is the natural rubber. Synthetic rubber can also be made and used in various ways.

Ruby

It is a valuable gemstone obtained from metamorphic rock. It is transparent red in colour which is a variety of the mineral corundum. It is precious than diamond. Industrial rubies have a variety of uses such as in watches, lasers, and other instruments.

Ruby

Runner

The term is used for the stem that horizontally grows to the ground from a creeping plant and turns into a new plant. It grows from the axillary or terminal buds, e.g. butter cup.

Rusting

The term refers to the corrosion of iron in which a layer of reddish-brown oxide of iron is formed as a result of an electrochemical process in the presence of oxygen and water. Iron undergoes rusting because of the presence of impurities in it and presence of acids or other electrolytes in the water.

Ryle, Sir Martin (1918-84)

He was a British Radio Astronomer who became Professor at Cambridge in 1959. He developed the technique of aperture synthesis. In 1974, he was awarded the Nobel Prize for Physics with Antony Hewish.

❑

Saccharin

It is a white crystalline solid derived from petroleum or coal tar. It is an artificial sweetener used as a substitute for sugar. It is 500 times sweeter than sugar. Its use is banned in some countries because of the presence of some carcinogenic substance in it.

Saline

It is used to refer a chemical compound which is salt or a solution containing salt.

Saliva

It refers to a fluid secreted by the salivary gland in the mouth. The fluid is alkaline in nature and it helps in the digestion of food because of the presence of an enzyme amylase which converts starch into sugar. Saliva also contains mucin which lubricates food and facilitates its passage into the stomach.

Salt

It is a compound formed as a result of the reaction of base and acid, in which the hydrogen of the acid is replaced by a metal. Salts are crystalline ionic compounds.

Sapwood

It is the outer layer of a tree or branch which conducts

water and gives structural support to the plant. It is xylem tissue.

Scattering

The term refers to the phenomenon in which the electromagnetic radiation gets deflected in the matter through which it passes because of the presence of particles there, for example, the scattering of the sunlight in the atmosphere because of the dust particles and air molecules there. The blue colour of the sky is due to the scattering of light.

Sclerosis

The term is used for the condition in which tissues or fibrosis becomes abnormally harder as in multiple sclerosis and arteriosclerosis.

Screen

In electronics, it refers to the flat surface which is actually an output device where information is displayed for the users. In portable computers liquid crystal display screens are commonly used while cathode ray tube is the most common type.

Scurvy

It is a disease, caused by the deficiency of vitamin C, with symptoms like weakness, bleeding of gums, dryness of skin and hair and pain in joints and muscles.

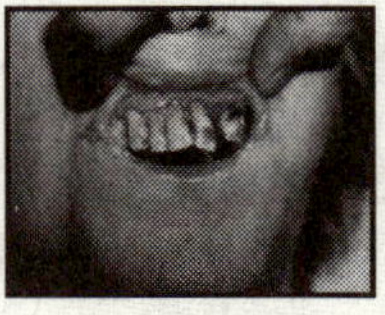

Scurvy

Sedative

The term is used for any drugs that induces soothing effect on the body and helps to relieve tension and anxiety. Its large doses reduce functional activity and induce sleep, e.g. narcotics.

Seed

It is the structure that develops from ovule after the fertilisation in angiosperms and gymnosperms. Seeds contain an embryo protected in a seed coat and food stored in endosperm or cotyledons. In angiosperms, the seeds are present in fruits while in gymnosperms they are naked but dormant state till suitable condition for germination.

Seismograph

It is a piece of equipment used to measure and record the strength of an earthquake, volcanic activity and explosions and other related information.

Semiconductor

It is a material which has electrical conductivity between that of an insulator and conductor. It means that it conducts electricity better than insulators but not as well as conductors, for example germanium, silicon and selenium. Semiconductors have varied uses such as in diodes, transistors, resistors, etc.

Sense organ

It refers to a cell, tissue or organ which is sensitive to external stimuli and can receive and respond accordingly. The sense organs are capable of detecting pleasure, pain, heat, pressure, etc. Eyes, nose, skin, ears and tongues are the example of sense organs.

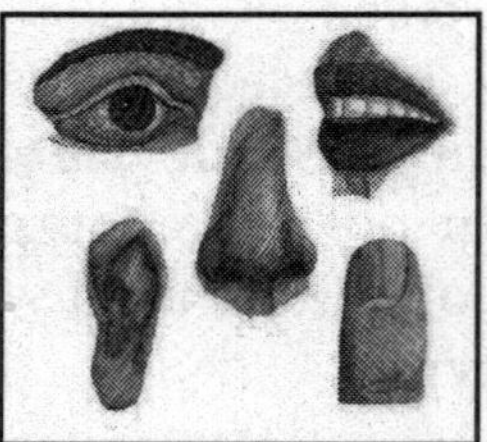

Sense organ

Sensor

It is a device which can react to heat, light and pressure to make a machine indicate an input signal. For example, a sensor in computer sends signals to indicate that the printer is short of paper while in a kiln it measures the temperature.

Shadow

It refers to an area of partial or complete darkness on the surface, caused when the source of light is blocked. When the source has a point, the shadow is sharply defined, but if the source is not a point, the shadow has two different regions — one is full shadow and the other is half shadow. The full shadow is called umbra and the half shadow is called penumbra.

Silicon (*Symbol* Si)

It is a metalloid element of in group 14 (formerly IVB) of the periodic table; atomic number 14; atomic weight 28.086; melting point 1410°C; boiling point 2355°C. Silicon is the second most abundantly found element in the earth's crust, constituting 25.7% by weight. It occurs in various forms such as silicon oxide and as silicon minerals. Silicon is a poor conductor of electricity, hence used in wires in telephones and telegraph and in transistors.

SI units

It refers to the international system of units widely used in all scientific purposes, replacing the c.g.s. and Imperial units. The system is based on the m.k.s. (meter, kilogram and second) and has seven basic units and two dimensionless units, also called supplementary units. Each unit has a symbol.

Skeleton

It is the structure of bones and cartilage which supports the body of human and animal. It protects the internal organs and serves as a framework for the muscles. The skeleton may be external or internal.

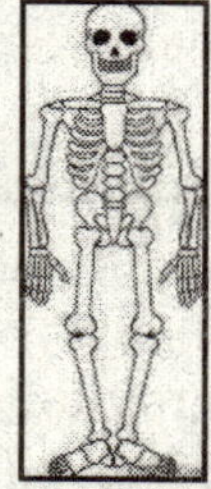

Skeleton

Skin

It is the natural outer layer of tissues which covers the body of the vertebrates. It consists of two layers – dermis and epidermis. Apart from protection, skin helps in maintaining body temperature, excretion of waste in the form of sweat and a store of fat. Besides, it is an important sense organ.

Sleeping sickness

It is a tropical disease transmitted by tsetse fly. Symptoms include fever, headache, loss of energy, drowsiness and swelling in the body. If it is not treated, it can be fatal.

Soft iron

It is a variety of iron which contains little amount of carbon but has high permeability. It can be magnetised and demagnetised easily and hysteresis loss is negligible. It is used in cores of electromagnets, transformers, motors and generators.

Solar energy

The term is used for the electromagnetic radiation coming to the earth from the sun. The total quantity of solar energy received by the earth in one year is about 4×10^{18} J while the total energy consumption of the earth for the same period is 3×10^{14} J. If harnessed, the sun can be a good source of energy on the earth.

Sound

It refers to a vibration in the range of 20 to 20000 Hertz which a human ear can hear. It is a form of energy transmitted by longitudinal waves. Sound travels in a medium which defines its speed. The velocity of sound in air is 332 meters per second.

Spiral galaxy

It refers to a collection of stars shaped like a disc with spiral arms, held together by the gravitational force. The Milky Way is an example of spiral galaxy.

Spiral galaxy

Spleen

It is a major organ in vertebrates located behind the stomach. It produces lymphocytes, antibodies, regulates the circulation of red blood cells in the body and destroys bacteria. It has a significant role in the defence mechanism of the body.

Star

The term is used for the celestial body which has high gas content and they produce energy by thermonuclear reaction or fusion of hydrogen into helium present there. They are self-luminous. The sun is our nearest star.

Steel

It is an alloy of iron, carbon, manganese, silicon, chromium, molybdenum and nickel in varying proportion. Steel with chromium is corrosion-free and rust-free and is called stainless steel. Steel is widely used in domestic field apart from medical and other fields.

Stethoscope

It is an instrument used by the doctors to listen the sounds of various internal organs, e.g. heart, lungs, etc. It helps in the diagnosis of heart, lungs diseases or chest infections.

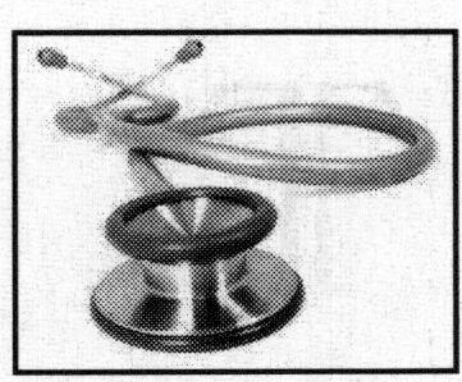
Stethoscope

Stratosphere

It is one of the layers of atmosphere next to troposphere extending up to 50 kms. The temperature is constant in this layer of the atmosphere.

Sun

It is a star at the centre of the solar system which at a distance of about 14,96,00,000 from the earth. It consists of 75% hydrogen and 25% helium. Its diameter is about 1392000 km and mass 1.9×10^{30} kg. The core temperature of the sun is about 1,00,00,000°C. Light takes eight minutes to reach the surface of the earth.

❑

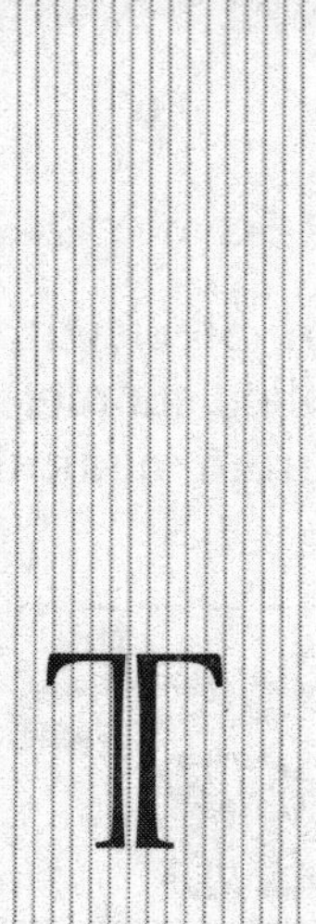

Tachograph

It is an instrument used to record the speed and the length of time of a moving vehicle. It is a combination of speedometer and clock.

Tachycardia

It is a condition of heart in which heart beat is rapid and abnormally high. It is caused by fever or excitement or arrhythmia. It is treated with specific drugs.

Tap root

It is the main root formed from the radical of the seed in dicot plants. It is the major support to the tall trees. In some plants like carrot, turnip, etc., tap roots are modified into storage roots.

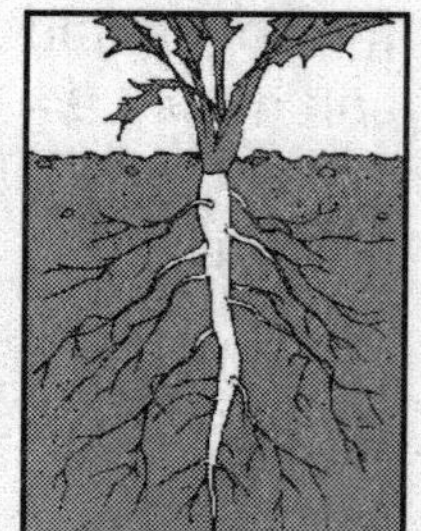

Tap root

Teflon

It is used for tetrafluoroethane which is highly resistant to heat, chemicals and wear. Hence, it is used as coating in non-stick cooking vessels, electrical insulations, bearing, etc.

Television

It refers to the reproduction of visual images by radio waves or cables. The image is first converted into electrical charges by the television camera, which is then scanned by electron beams, producing electrical signals of the picture. These signals are broadcast as electromagnetic waves and picked by the TV aerials to be fed into the receiver i.e. TV sets.

Temperature

It refers to the intensity of heat of a body, usually measured in degree Celsius, Kelvin or Fahrenheit.

Tensiometer

It is a device used to measure the surface tension of a liquid. It is also used for measuring the moisture content of soil. The device measures the tension in a wire too.

Test tube baby

The term is used for a baby that grows from an egg and fertilized outside the mother's body, usually in a scientific tube, and then put back inside the uterus for further development. Hence, it is called test tube baby.

Tetanus

It is a serious infection caused by a bacteria *Clostridium tetani* which enters into the body through wounds. The bacteria produce toxin which causes muscle spam and lock jaw. If not treated on time, it can be fatal.

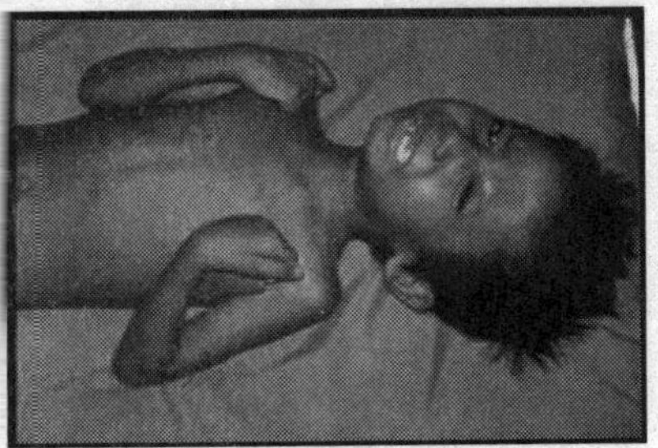

Tetanus

Thermodynamics

It is a branch of Science which studies the relations between heat and other forms of energy.

Thiamine

It is a vitamin of B-complex group, present in liver, yeast, grains, eggs, etc. Its deficiency causes beriberi, a disease which affects the nervous system. It is also called vitamin B1.

Thyroid gland

It refers to the largest of the endocrine glands in vertebrates, situated in the base of the throat. It secretes two hormone thyroxin and triodothyronine, which contain iodine. These two hormones control the rate of metabolism in the body and have significant role in physical growth and activity of the nervous system.

Tissue

The term is used for a collection of similar cells, forming the different parts of plants and organisms, doing the same function. There are different types of tissues like connective tissues, nervous tissues, muscular tissues, etc.

Tonsil

It is a mass of paired lymphoid tissue, based at the back of the mouth in vertebrates. Tonsils produce lymphocytes and defend the body against infections.

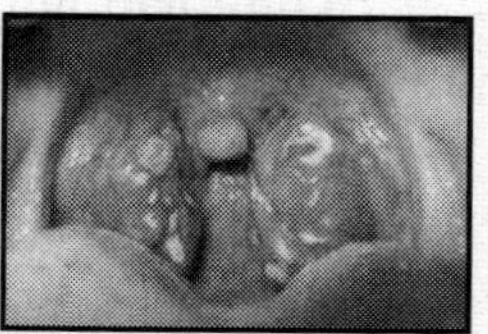

Tonsil

Torr

It is a unit of pressure in high vacuum technology. It is equal to 133.322 Pascal.

Toxicology

The term is used for the study of poisons and their effects on living organisms.

Transformer

It is a device which converts alternating current of one voltage to another, without a change in frequency, by electromagnetic induction.

Translucent

The term refers to the phenomenon in which the passage of light is permitted, though there is some scattering and diffusion, so that the object cannot be seen clearly, e.g. frosted glass.

Triple vaccine

It is a combination of three vaccines to provide protection against diphtheria, whooping cough and tetanus. The dose has to be repeated and the booster dose is followed with it.

Twins

The term is used for two individuals born at the same time to the same mother, developed either from the same egg or two separately fertilized eggs.

Twins

Typhus

It is an infectious disease which causes high fever, headache and skin eruptions. It is spread by lice. Sulpha drugs and antibiotics are used to cure it.

❑

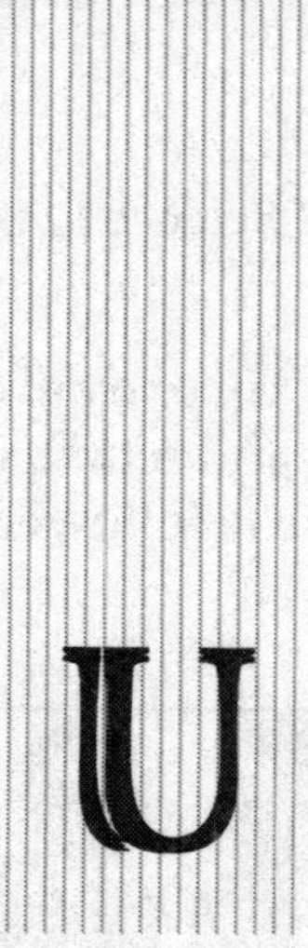

Ubiquinone

The term refers to a quinine-derived compound which serves as electron carrier in different biochemical reaction in the body.

Ulna

The term is used for the longer two bones in the forelimb of the vertebrates which is joined with the carpals at the wrist and humerus at the elbow joint.

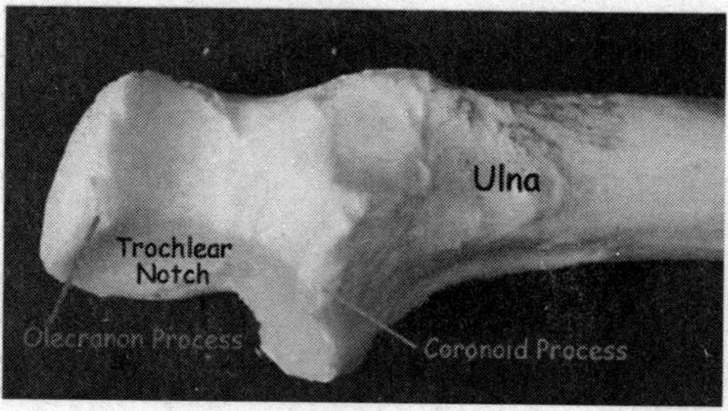

Ulna

Ultrasonic

It refers to the study and use of sound waves which have a frequency above 20000 Hz and are beyond human ear. Ultrasonics are used in medicine and for diagnosis, particularly pre-natal, as a substitute for the X-ray which could have harmful effect, besides industry and others.

Ultraviolet radiation

It is the electromagnetic radiation with wavelengths in the range between 400 nanometres and 4 nanometres, i.e. violet light and long X-rays. The sun is a major source of ultraviolet radiation but much of the radiation is absorbed by the ozone layer.

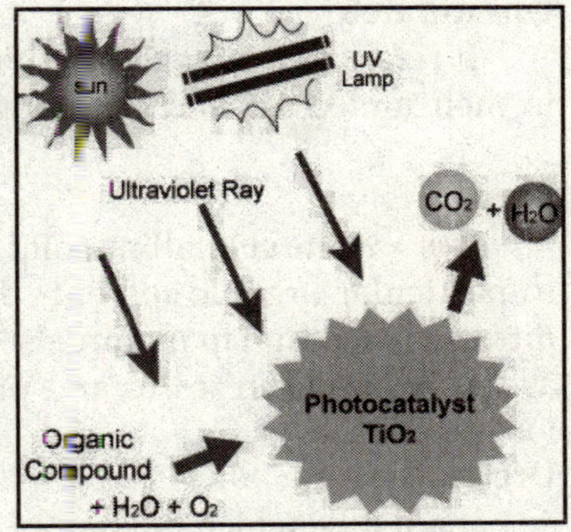

Ultraviolet radiation

Unicellular

It is used for organisms which are composed of a single cell, e.g. protozoa, bacteria, fungi, etc.

Unisexual

The term refers to plants or organisms with either male or female sex, but not both. Many evolved animals are unisexual. There are unisexual flowers with either stamens or carpals.

Unit

The term is used to denote the specified measure of a physical quantity, e.g. time, length, mass, etc. Now, all systems have been replaced by the SI unit for all scientific purposes.

Universal donor

The term is used for persons with blood group O which has no agglutinogen. Hence, they can donate blood to any group because this O group has no clumping or agglutination.

Universal recipient

It refers to persons with AB blood group which has no agglutinin in their blood. Hence, they can receive blood from person of any group.

Unsaturated

It refers to a substance which has double or triple bonds in their molecules and can undergo additional reaction.

Urea

It is a white crystalline solid, soluble in water but insoluble in particular organic solvents. It is the main end, product of nitrogen excretion in mammals. Urea is synthesised to be used as fertilizer and in resins and pharmaceuticals.

Ureter

It is a tube which is a part of the urinary system in animals. It takes urine from the kidney to the bladder in vertebrates.

Urethra

It is the tube which takes urine from the bladder to be disposed outside the body. In males, it serves as a channel for semen.

Urine

It is an aqueous fluid filtered out by the excretory organs formed as a result of metabolic process. It consists of water, salts, proteins and nitrogenous wastes, e.g. urea, uric acid, creatinine, ammonia, etc. In humans, urine is produced by the kidneys. Urine output varies in various animals. A healthy human produces average 1 to 1.5 litre urine per day.

USB drive

The term is usually used for a storage device which can be connected to a computer through a special connection. They are widely used for back-up, data transfer and storage of images.

USB drive

❑

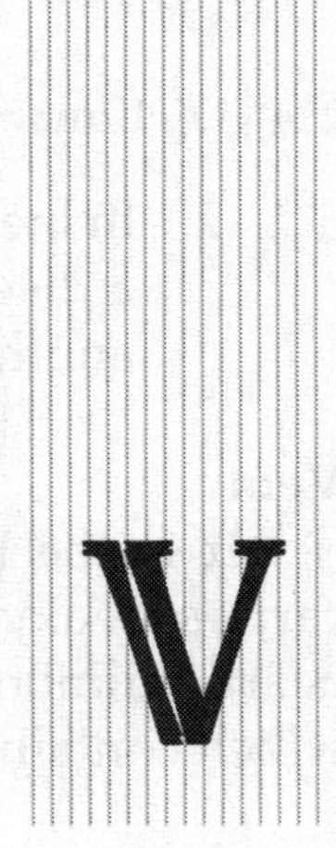

Vaccination

It refers to a process by which an individual's immunity is enhanced by giving them a dose of weak bacteria or virus or their toxins, either orally or by injection, which stimulate the production of antibodies in the blood, e.g. polio vaccine.

Vacuum flask

Vacuum flask

It is a flask which prevents the loss of heat by radiation, convection and conduction which helps to keep things either hot or cold.

Vapour

The term is used for a gas which is obtained when the state of a liquid or solid is changed on being heated.

Vascular system

The term is used for the network of tubes through which fluids circulate in the body tissues. In all animals, there is a vascular system for the flow of nutrients and other things like wastes.

Vector

It denotes the following:

1. In physics, it refers to a quantity which has both magnitude and direction, e.g. force.

2. In medical, the term is used for an insect which carries a disease-causing organism from one living thing to another.

Vein

It is the blood vessel which usually carries deoxygenated blood towards the heart, pulmonary vein being an exception which contains pure blood.

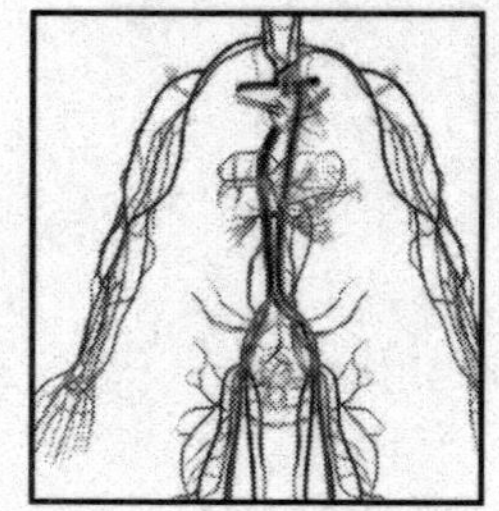

Vein

Virology

It relates to the scientific study of viruses, including their structure and genetic make-up.

Virus

In microbiology, it refers to an infectious particle which is too small to be seen with a microscope. Viruses are parasites of plants, animals and bacteria and they become active only when they are inside a host. Viruses cause disease like influenza, polio, AIDS, hepatitis, small pox, etc.

In computer, it is a program or part of a program which can make copies of itself and transfer itself from one computer to another without the operator being aware of it. Usually, viruses are designed to damage the data.

Viscosity

It is the resistance of a fluid to flow caused by internal friction when the fluid is subjected to shear stress. Its SI unit is Pascal second.

Vitamin

It is a vital organic compounds required by living organisms in small quantity for normal growth and development and maintenance of health and fitness. There are 14 major vitamins some of which are soluble in fat while some in water; for example , B-complex and vitamin C are water soluble and vitamins A, D, E and K are soluble in fat. Plants and animals are sources of most of vitamins B and vitamin C.

Volt (*Symbol* V)

It is the SI unit of electromotive force which is defined as the difference of potential between two points on a conductor carrying a constant current of one ampere with one watt power.

Voltaic cell

It is a device which produces an emf from the chemical reactions within it. It occurs because of two electrodes dipped into an electrolyte.

Voluntary muscle

These are the muscles controlled by the will and attached to the skeleton. They consist of striated muscle fibres and help in movement. They are also called skeletal muscles.

Vulcanisation

It is a process which makes rubber hard when it is heated with sulphur. The rubber loses its elasticity and becomes hard depending on the percentage of sulphur.

Vulcanisation

❑

Warfarin

It is a synthetic anticoagulant used in medicine, and in lethal doses to kill rodents.

Water

It is a tasteless, colourless liquid, boiling point 100°C and freezing point 0°C. It is vital for life on the earth. About 70% of the earth is covered with water while about 60% to 70% of the human body consists of water. Its chemical formula is H_2O.

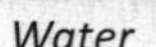

Water

Water gas

It is a mixture of carbon monoxide and hydrogen. It is produced by passing steam over hot coke. It is a fuel gas and was mainly used in the past for producing ammonia.

Watt (*Symbol* W)

It is the SI unit of power which is defined as a power of one joule per second.

Wave

It is a periodic disturbance occurring in a medium or space. Waves have properties like wavelength, speed, frequency and amplitude. There are two types of waves – longitudinal wave and transverse wave.

Wave power

It refers to the use of wave power in the sea for the generation of electricity. It has immense potential to be harnessed as an inexhaustible source of energy.

Weight

It refers to the force exerted by the earth to attract a body towards it. The weight of an object depends on the mass and strength of the gravitational pull of the earth. Hence, an object weighs heavier at the poles than the equator with the same mass.

Whales

It belongs to the group of aquatic mammals, including the blue whales which are 30 meters long having weight about 130 tonnes. They have a thick layer of fat all over their body which is called blubber. Their fore limbs are modified into flippers.

Whales

White blood cell

It is a colourless cell produced in the lymph nodes and bone marrow. They produce antibodies and help in fighting against a disease. They add to the immunity of the body.

Whooping cough

It is an acute form of contagious disease largely affecting children. It is caused by a bacteria called *Bordetella pertussis.* Symptoms include wild attack of cough accompanied with whoops and often fever. Preventive vaccination is available against the disease.

Wilson's disease

It is an inborn metabolical disorder in which there is a deficiency of ceruloplasmin. Free copper gets deposited in the liver or brain causing jaundice or mental retardation respectively. Regular dose of penicillamine helps to cure the disease.

Wind power

Wind power

The term is used to denote the use of wind to drive machinery or produce electricity. Wind power has the potential to generate about 10^{20} J of energy per year throughout the world. It can be a good source of renewable energy.

Wood

It refers to hard structural fibrous tissues forming trunks and branches of many perennial trees, shrubs and plants. It is composed of secondary xylem and associated fibres. The wood of angiosperms is called hard wood, e.g. oak, and that of gymnosperms is called softwood, for example, fir.

Work

It is defined as the amount of energy transfer to a system to make an object move. Work is equal to the product of force applied and the distance moved in the direction of the force.

Wrought iron

It is the one of the purest forms of iron which contains slag only 1-3%. It rusts less readily compared to other forms of iron and welds easily. It is used in manufacturing of chains, tubes, hooks, etc.

❑

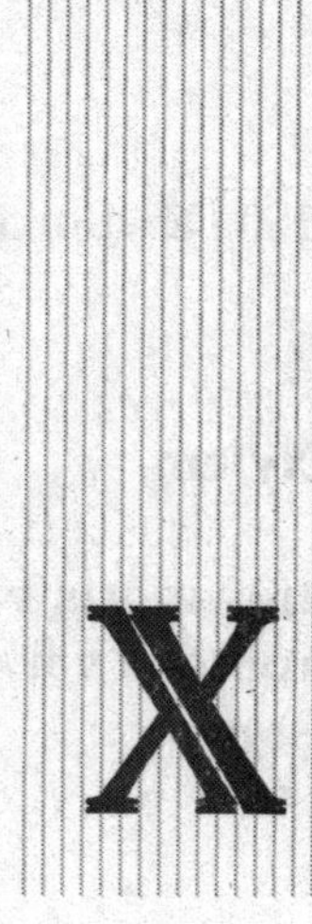

Xanthophyll

It is an oxygen-containing pigment which gives yellow and brown colour to the autumn leaves.

Xenon (*Symbol* Xe)

It is a colourless, odourless gas of group 18 of the periodic table, atomic number 54; atomic weight 1131.30; melting point - 111.9°C; boiling point: - 107.1°C. It is present in the atmosphere in small quantity (0.00087%). It is used in fluorescent lamp and bubble chambers

Xerophytes

The term is used for the plants which are adapted to survive in very dry conditions. They have fleshy green stems, spines, thick cuticles and absence of leaves which all help them to survive in such dry conditions. Cacti are the examples of xerophytes.

Xerophytes

X-ray

It refers to the band of electromagnetic radiation with wavelength in the range of 10^{-11} to 10^{-9} meters which is actually the range between gamma rays and ultraviolet radiation. X-rays are highly penetrating hence used in diagnosis of diseases.

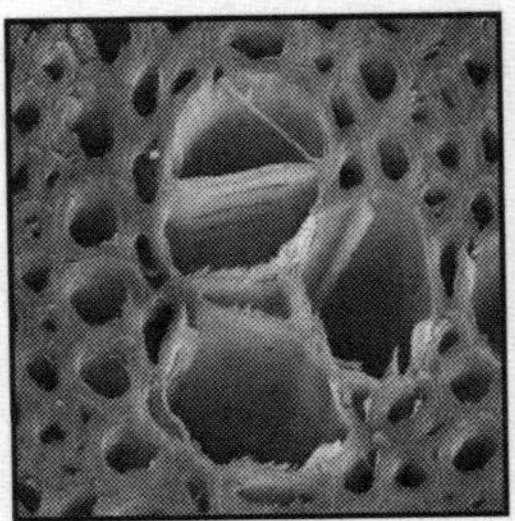
Xylem

Xylem

It is a tissue in vascular plants which transports water and minerals from the roots to various parts such as leaves and stems.

Yagi aerial

It is a directional aerial array, consisting of one or more diapoles, a parabolic reflector and a series of closely spaced directors. It is widely used for radio and television telescope.

Yard

It is the former Imperial standard unit of length equal to 3 feet (36 inches) or approximately 91.4 centimeters.

Yeast

It belongs to a group of unicellular fungi. They convert sugar solutions into alcohol and cause fermentation, hence widely used in baking and brewing industries.

Yellow fever

It is an infectious tropical disease transmitted by mosquitoes. It is called yellow fever because it makes the skin turn yellow with symptoms of fever, headache, etc. It is a viral disease which can be prevented by vaccination.

Yolk

It is the part of egg which stores food consisting of protein, fats, lipid, etc. to be used for the developing embryos. The yolk is relatively large in the eggs of the bird.

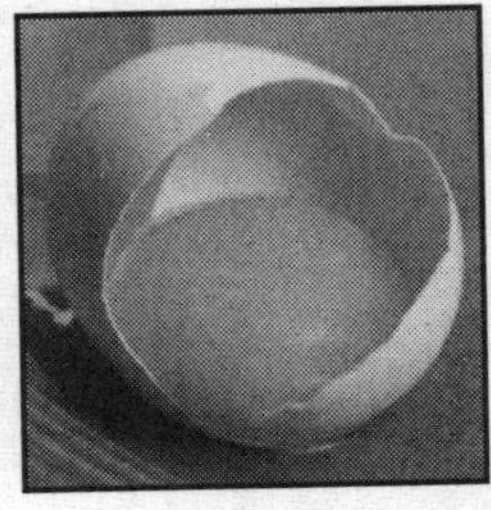

Yolk

Ytterbium (*Symbol* Yb)

It is a silvery white metallic element, belonging to the lanthanoids, atomic number 70; atomic weight 173.04; melting point 819°C; boiling point: 1194°C. It occurs in gadolinite, monazite and xenotime. It is used in steel.

Ytterbium

❑

Zeolite

It refers to hydrated aluminium silicate with three-dimensional crystal structure. Zeolite can be natural or synthetic. Zeolites are used for separating mixtures, hence used in molecular sieves. They are also used in water-softening.

Zinc (*Symbol* Zn)

It is a bluish-white metallic element, atomic number 30; atomic weight 65.88; melting point 419.88°C; boiling point 907°C. It occurs as zinc blende. Its alloys are brass and bronze. It is used in galvanising. It is a reactive metal.

Zinc

Zirconium (Symbol Zr)

It is a greyish white metallic transition element, atomic number 40; atomic weight 91.22; melting point: 1852°C; boiling point 4377°C. It occurs in zircon and zinc oxide. It is used in steel manufacturing, ceramics, fuel cell, etc. It is also used in nuclear reactors.

Zygomatic arch

The term is used for the arch bones below the eyes, on both sides of the face.

Zygote

It is the fertilized cell formed when the male reproductive cell join the female reproductive cell. It is the stage prior to the embryo. This cell develops into a young one.

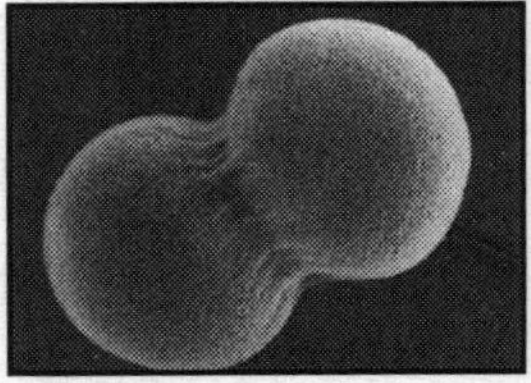

Zygote

❑❑❑